Write Dance in the Early Years
Second Edition

A Lucky Duck Book

Write Dance in the Early Years
Second Edition

Ragnhild A. Oussoren

Translated by Rosemary Mitchell-Schuitevoerder

Los Angeles | London | New Delhi
Singapore | Washington DC

This edition first published 2010
First edition published 2005, reprinted in 2006, 2007, 2008 (twice), 2009

First published 2004, Netherlands

SAGE Publications
1 Oliver's Yard
55 City Road
London EC1Y 1SP

SAGE Publications Inc.
2455 Teller Road
Thousand Oaks, California 91320

SAGE Publications India Pvt Ltd
B 1/I 1 Mohan Cooperative Industrial Area
Mathura Road, Post Bag 7
New Delhi 110 044

SAGE Publications Asia-Pacific Pte Ltd
3 Church Street
#10-04 Samsung Hub
Singapore 049483

Library of Congress Control Number 2009937944

British Library Cataloguing in Publication data
A catalogue record for this book is available from the British Library

ISBN 978-1-84920-138-4
ISBN 978-1-84920-139-1 (pbk)

Typeset by SAGE
Printed on paper from sustainable resources
Printed in Great Britain by Ashford Colour Press Ltd, Gosport, Hampshire

MIX
Paper from
responsible sources
FSC
www.fsc.org   FSC® C011748

For my three grandchildren Oliver, Barnaby and Freya
who taught me how to be Bestemor (grandma)

Contents

Themes, Stories and Arrangement of the CD

Home		pag.	CD no.	CD instr.	
Home 1	Sandy Hill	26	1	2	DVD
Home 2	Kringeli-Krangeli	32	3	4	DVD
Home 3	Pat-a-cake	38	5	6	DVD
Home 4	The Staircase	44	7	8	DVD
Home 5	The Toy Train	50	9	10	DVD
Home 6	Tickle Tree	56	11	12	
Home 7	Little Water Shute	62	13	14	
Home 8	The Rainbow	68	15	16	DVD
Home 9	Little Sun	74	17	18	
Home 10	Straight, Bent, Cross, Happy	80	19,21,23,25	20,22,24,26	DVD

Contents

Themes, Stories and Arrangement of the CD

Write Dance in the Early Years is a movement-based programme designed to develop children's gross and fine motor co-ordination starting from their own emotions and natural movements. Movement plays a central role in learning to write. Until basic whole body movements have been mastered the brain is unable to transfer these actions into the fine motor skills required for writing. Correct letter formation cannot be achieved until the basic whole body writing movement is smooth, flowing, controlled and performed with self-confidence.

Modern society has brought many changes to all our lives and young, pre-school children in particular have very different experiences to those of children born just 20 or 30 years ago. Although these changes are stimulating and exciting; electronic games, computers, baby walkers, battery powered tricycles etc, in many ways they have reduced some of the essential physical activities that developed many of the pre-writing skills in children. Children nowadays spend much less time outdoors, skipping, pedalling cycles, playing ball and their indoor play invariably involves toys that need buttons pressed, but require little physical manipulation. Many children have had limited access to cutting and painting prior to pre-school, preferring the light and noise stimulation of electronic games. As a result children arrive in school demonstrating significantly less developed whole body coordination, rhythm, wrist strength and control and as a result find holding and controlling writing and drawing tools difficult.

Write Dance was written following a study in Northern Europe, investigating the reasons for the changes in children's pre-writing skills. All the movements, actions and drawings in the Write Dance programme are carefully planned to provide the whole body experiences essential to filling in the 'missing gaps' in movement and coordination development, thus enabling children to become confident, fluent and willing writers.

Write Dance in the Early Years does not teach letter formation. It uses music, rhythm, story, song, rhyme, sensory play and dance to teach the essential skills necessary for handwriting. These include:

- Co-ordination
- Rhythm
- Wrist strength and flexibility
- Balance between tension and relaxation
- Flowing, angular, circular movements
- Control of speed and direction of movements
- Control of pressure
- Concentration

Writing is a developmental process and trying to encourage children to form defined letters using the correct formation before they have the necessary whole body movement and coordination is setting them up to experience failure and to become reluctant writers. Children need to move sequentially through the different stages of development in order to become successful writers. By ensuring children's whole body movements are fully developed before teaching formal handwriting skills, children avoid experiencing early feelings of inadequacy and failure. The correct delivery of *Write Dance in the Early Years* not only enables children to practise and develop these essential skills, it also enables them to experiment with a wide range of mark making tools.

Write Dance in the Early Years supports The Early Years Foundation Stage Principles: A Unique Child; Positive Relationships; Enabling Environments; and Learning and Development. The hands on experimental nature of the songs, 'scrimbling' and theme play also supports the Early Years Foundation Stage philosophy of child-centred learning in a practical, linked and meaningful curriculum. The 'Theme Play' encourages children to engage in imaginative play whilst supporting the development of whole body movement and co-ordination. Themes link easily to Foundation Stage cross-curricular topics.

Children participating in *Write Dance in the Early Years* will be working towards Foundation Stage objectives across all six areas of learning and development.

Creative Development: Every theme within *Write Dance in the Early Years* includes a song, encouraging children to participate in singing simple songs from memory. Children relate quickly to the characters in the stories and respond imaginatively in theme-play. They develop a sense of rhythm during the whole body movement and when 'scrimbling' to music.

Physical Development: The whole body movements within each theme of *Write Dance in the Early Years* provide opportunities to develop the skills to move with confidence, showing control, co-ordination and an awareness of space. The 'scrimbling' and theme play activities encourage the handling of tools, objects and materials with control and develop gross and fine motor control. As all the activities are linked to music and song, *Write Dance in the Early Years* also develops rhythm, coordination and balance.

Knowledge and Understanding of the World: Children are encouraged to experience and experiment with a variety of tools and materials through 'scrimbling' in a variety of media: shaving foam, paint, sand, rice, flour, clay etc. The theme play can readily be linked to the development of children's knowledge and understanding of the world around them.

Communication, Language and Literacy: The engaging characters and stories within *Write Dance in the Early Years* encourage children to listen with enjoyment to stories and songs and to use language to imagine and recreate roles in 'theme play'. Through 'scrimbling', children develop the fine motor skills required for handwriting, enabling them to hold and control different writing tools to successfully form recognisable letters.

Mathematical Development: The songs and stories in *Write Dance in the Early Years* provide opportunities for children to recite number names in order, count objects and actions and to use the language of direction, simple shapes and discuss patterns.

Personal, Social and Emotional Development: Including Write Dance in the early years setting will provide opportunities for children to select and use activities and resources independently, develop their confidence to try new ideas, encourage them to work co-operatively as part of a group, sharing resources, space etc. and to express feelings in appropriate ways. *Write Dance in The Early Years* encourages children to participate in a range of activities that ensure children experience a sense of success and achievement.

As part of The Every Child Matters Agenda schools are actively concerned with promoting enjoyment and achievement and the development of health and safety with all their children, ensuring they are equipped to succeed in society throughout their lifetime. As a Write Dance practitioner and trainer I have experienced the enjoyment and motivation that the materials provide for both the children and the adults involved in the teaching and learning of preschool and foundation stage children, developing self-confidence, motivation and participation. Children quickly learn the different movements to each song and participate eagerly. The short, daily delivery of the whole body movements encourages daily exercise and activity, supporting the development of an active lifestyle. These short, physical sessions are particularly effective when delivered by teachers at times during the day when they require the children to refocus and concentrate.

Despite the ever developing technical world that we live in, being able to communicate effectively using writing will always be important in securing and succeeding both in employment and every day life. Making the early development of writing skills a positive and enjoyable experience for children is crucial if children are to become confident, able writers.

Write Dance in the Early Years is a medium for providing an exciting introduction to writing for young children and developing positive attitudes towards writing.

Hilary Thompson
Assistant Head Teacher, Nansen Primary School, Birmingham

Once upon a time there was a piece of paper.

'I am so lonely,' said the piece of paper, 'and I look so white, why won't anybody come and play with me?' The piece of paper was lying on the kitchen table and was very bored. Then Yoyo came into the kitchen to have a drink of squash and the piece of paper began to call Yoyo softly.

'Yoyo, come here! Look, I am a piece of paper!'
Yoyo didn't hear and so the piece of paper began to call a little louder.

'Yoyo, come HERE!' it shouted. 'Look, I am a piece of paper!' but Yoyo still didn't hear.
Next Meema came into the kitchen to have a drink of squash and when the door opened the piece of paper fell on the floor. The piece of paper continued to call out.

'Yoyo, come here, I am a piece of paper!'
This time Meema did hear it and she said to Yoyo:

'Did you hear that Yoyo? I think the piece of paper is calling you.'
Yoyo and Meema knelt down and put their ears close to the piece of paper. They both clearly heard what the piece of paper was saying.

'Thank you, oh thank you so much, would you mind colouring me, I am so white and naked.'
Yoyo and Meema quickly went to fetch their box of crayons and began to scrimble all kinds of things on the piece of paper. They now heard the piece of paper starting to giggle and laugh because the colouring and squiggling of the crayons and pencils tickled. Yoyo and Meema turned it into a real piece of art. Finally Meema said:

'Dear little piece of paper, are you happy now?'

'Yes, thank you, oh thank you so much, now make me fly quickly!' Yoyo folded the paper into a wonderful plane and sent it flying through the room.

'Oops!' They heard the paper say. 'It tickles in my tummy', and crash … it tumbled into the plants.

'Once more Yoyo, I want to fly again,' called the piece of paper from the plant box.

Well, Yoyo and Meema continued to play for hours and hours with the piece of paper they had coloured themselves. It landed under the table and on top of the cupboard, on the counter with its tip near the jam jar ('Wow, delicious!' they heard it say), on the stove, next to the cat litter and last of all… in the sink, which had a little bit of water at the bottom.

'Oh dear, oh no, now I can no longer fly,' said the piece of paper sadly, but Yoyo lifted it out carefully, and put it down on the windowsill and spoke gently.

'Don't worry, dear little pretty coloured piece of paper, tomorrow your wings will have dried again and we will play with you. Go to sleep now, it is dark. Sleep well…' and Yoyo and Meema closed the door of the kitchen quietly.

What about the piece of paper? It fell asleep straightaway; it was exhausted after all that flying!

Introduction

1. What is Write Dance?

Write Dance is a handwriting methodology and handwriting method designed for all children in primary and early years education, including children with special educational needs, learning difficulties or disabilities. Write Dance tries to teach children to write starting from their own emotions and natural movements, giving it their own 'swing'. Creating movements from their own emotions is of prime importance. A good shape, a 'beautiful' letter, cannot be created until the basic movement is smooth and flowing and performed with enough self-confidence. For example, Write Dance encourages children to feel what a letter 'o' is like, to hear it and experience it before they actually begin to write it. That is why we practise the movements live and in our spaces. Only then do we 'scrimble', 'write draw' and write on board, paper or any other writing surface. Writing movements made to sounds, noises and music help the 'o' to become and remain rounded, so that the children will eventually know how to make it smaller, without having to force themselves and without feeling pushed, and without forcing the shape or pressing too hard on their writing utensils. Only then can they write a beautifully rounded and healthy 'o', and this 'o' will become their personal 'o'.

Write Dance and music, songs, rhymes and games are inseparable. Through this play, the basic movements become automatic and are stored in the motor centre in the brain so that initial writing can be performed without forced effort and frustration and can provide on-going pleasure. All the actions in the Write Dance programme are concentrated on making the children feel happy and comfortable with their bodies. They cannot make mistakes; any expression is a good expression, even if the paper is torn up, crumpled up or thrown away angrily. Such behaviour isn't wrong either, because all the child is doing is getting rid of her frustrations! Write Dance offers plenty of opportunities for movements to come naturally, drawing upon emotional experiences and linking to a child's own fantasy world, which is the best way to encourage children's learning. Write Dance focuses on the child, and their inner experiences continue to be its primary guideline.

2. Write Dance in the Early Years

The unique features of Write Dance, its child-centredness and its appeal to emotions that are immediately expressed in movements without the need to achieve or perform, make it ideally suited to start with children at a very early age. That is why this publication of *Write Dance in the Early Years* should be seen as a complete re-draft of Write Dance (written for four to eight year olds), adjusted entirely to the pre-school age group. *Write Dance in the Early Years* contains nine themes, each one with a 'Home' and a 'Funfair' alternative. Certain basic movements will be central to each theme and will continue to be developed in two ways, once in Home and once in Funfair. You will find a more comprehensive summary in the tables at the beginning of this book. There is a song on the CD for both the Home and Funfair alternatives. All the songs have been composed specifically for Write Dance in the Early Years. There is also an instrumental version of each song on the CD. For each theme in the programme, the book contains an introductory story and the lyrics of the song, including suggestions for 'Movements in Your Spaces' and 'Scrimbling'. There are also sections called 'Theme Play' with ideas for games and working with sensory materials.

3. Movements in Your Space

Most movements can be performed standing, walking, sitting or even lying down. Usually there will also be an alternative to 'walking movements' available which allows the children to sit. The teacher will not find the simple lyrics and tunes of the songs and accompanying descriptions of movements in their spaces difficult. Initially the movements will feel a bit strange to some of the children, which does not matter. Firstly it is important to initiate general movements by listening, seeing, imitating, experiencing and doing them. Initially, you can leave the music off and practice the basic movements (such as walking straight or bent, turning wrists or hands) several times in succession, accompanied by your own noises, sounds or words.
Children who do not want to join in at all are allowed to watch, lie on the floor, 'thrash about' or move in their own time. Generally a child will join in after a while of their own accord. It is no use forcing them. This has never been the intention of write dancing. Getting children to move their entire bodies is always good preparation for scrimbling or writing movements on self-made boards, paper or any other writing surfaces. While moving on their writing surface, it is not at all surprising to see children's movements evolve spontaneously, with arms going up in the air, or children standing up, walking or dancing.

4. Movements on a Scrimbling Surface

'Scrimbling' is a word coined for Write Dance and means working on a writing surface by:
> • scribbling
> • stippling (making dots and dashes on the paper using the end of a paint brush. In Write Dance, we can also use our fingers or another instrument)
> • wriggling
> • doodling
> • circling
> • experiencing and experimenting.

The children will scrimble with a scrimbling instrument on a scrimbling surface, where both instrument and surface should be taken in the broadest sense. For instance, 'finger dancing' is scrimbling with your fingers, straight on the table top or on the board, or on their own bodies first and then, for example, on somebody else's back. Finger dancing over 'scrimbles' which have just been completed in chalk will encourage recognition and can be a practical way of starting revision. The German word 'Fingerspitzengefühl', meaning the intuitive feeling at your finger tips, refers to the signals that are being sent to the big programme in your brain. We like to offer the children a great variety of scrimbling tools and scrimbling surfaces.

5. Both Hands

Just like we do in 'write drawing' in the book, *Write Dance*, we will 'scrimble' as much as possible with both hands. This comes naturally to pre-school children and it stimulates the two halves of our brain. The left and right hemispheres have different functions which we will need all our lives. Left or right-handedness starts to develop after the second year, which is known as 'lateralisation', however we should give pre-school children the opportunity to use both hands as laterality is not always fully developed until much later. Moving around in their spaces will make using both hands very easy and we will immediately notice if there are any problems and where there might be difficulties with motor skills development in the future.

6. Consolidating or reinforcing

Basic movements on the writing surface may be expressed slowly or quickly, big or small, with strong or gentle pressure, round or straight and so on. We always try to do this using as many colours as possible. The repetition of movement in different colours over each other is called 'consolidating' in typical Write Dance terminology. We could compare it with a river that has been running down the rocks for years, streaming or thundering and cutting out a shape. In the same way scrimbling will create personal shapes (and eventually letters) by means of 'the personal swing' a child attaches to her movements. This personal 'swing' is established by repeatedly practising hand-eye co-ordination: a child will perceive with her eyes what is happening on the writing surface, feel and experience it with her hand(s) and hear the accompanying sounds, noises and music. Consolidating or reinforcing in child language means doing and repeating the movements over each other, with their own swing and the momentum of successive moments – in other words, NO tracing!

7. Experiencing and Emotions

Writing is intrinsically related to emotions. This link is perhaps most apparent when the emotions are blocked. The shapes of the letters cannot be created smoothly and in a flowing style. They will have 'frozen', which becomes apparent when we see the children pressing too hard on their writing utensils, and consequently producing impulsive unintentional strokes, closed letters, the abrupt breaking off of letters and words and sentences too close to each other. However, if the emotions can be freed the rest will follow and, most of all, self-confidence will return. This self-confidence is an inexhaustible source for creativity, games and social and motor skills, but also for dealing with new learning experiences. Even though scrimbling doesn't initially need to 'mesh' with the music, the movements, converted into a splash of colours on the page, will provide you with a picture of the young child's perception of their environment. These drawings done to music will represent expressions or reflections of the child's mood and developing personality. The more variation children can use to express them-selves through basic movements - for example cheerfully and angrily, forcefully and carefully, firmly and relaxed, messily and beautifully - the more freely they will be able to move on a smaller writing surface.

8. Repetition and Routine

The repetition of movements, routines and rituals, the re-telling of stories or fairy tales, and the singing of the same songs again and again will give a young child, including a child with developmental delay or difficulties, a sense of trust and safety, and in this lies the strength of the repetition process. Repetitions are fundamental to the development of the skills acquired through Write Dance across a wider area. If you know the words, songs, dance steps, scales and exercises by heart, you will be ready to come up with variations and to let your imagination loose. 'Being different' or 'being silly' may have positive results, allowing the child to acquire a strong sense of contrasting emotions or expressions. It is fun to scrimble on the board, but even more fun to do so with your feet and your nose. The revision activities we choose to perform need to remain challenging and should fit in with the child's world of movements. Therefore we will always perform the basic movements in our spaces in the same way, but each time it will be a new situation, a new day or a new week in another season and thus it will offer us new experiences. We will always give the child enough time to say what they feel and experience, both in their bodies and in their expressions on the writing surface.

9. Development

Once the child has got used to scrimbling, it could become a daily reoccurring activity, available whenever they feel like it and feel safe and secure using the writing surface. The older the child, the more they will be able to control their movements in their spaces and on their writing surfaces. They will feel they have mastered their 'controls' and that is when the teacher or parent/carer should step back from encouraging the child to produce beautiful, representational or 'perfect' shapes. In a society in which we are constantly trying to hit targets, it might seem incongruous that initially we want to reduce regulations and pressure, and the corresponding muscular efforts. Heavy pressure on a pencil produces a deeper colour which 'proves' you can produce a shape. The opposite, that is applying less pressure and repeating the movements over each other, has a healing effect in our lives today.

10. The Scrimbling Area

Preferably this should be a permanent area with a self-made board attached to the wall with one or two separate boards within reach, ready to be put on the table. It is possible to paint a table with chalkboard paint, which can be used as a Write Dance table. A tray with pieces of chalk and a tray with small pieces of sponge should be included. In addition there should be rolls of wallpaper, large sheets of paper, pieces of chalk and possibly other materials, for example, a tray with play sand. Of course a CD-player will be needed to play the audio CD.

11. Materials for the Writing Surface

Boards

Use sheets of MDF cut to size (for example, 1022 x 600mm), so that the children can work side by side or opposite each other, or half the size, suitable for one child. The thickness could be 4 or 6mm. Paint both sides with chalkboard paint (any colour). Usually it is sufficient to pass over it once or twice with a roller of paint on the front and back. It is also possible to paint lines or waves for a special effect on some boards. The boards can be held in place with non-slip mats, but that might not be necessary. Blu-Tac could help stick them down to the table, too.

Small tables

It is always possible to scrimble with hands and fingers on the clear top of a child's table. It is what we call finger dancing.

Write Dance table

This is an ordinary rectangular or round (old) table painted with chalkboard paint and it is always available for the child to scrimble on. The legs of the table are cut off at child height. A hole can be cut out with a diameter of about 450 mm in the centre of the round table, big enough for one child to stand in where they can scrimble around themselves. If you stand in the middle you will be the centre of attention and play an important part. It also helps the child to find their bearings in a circle.

Tip: You might be able to buy an old coffee table in a second hand shop for very little money. These tables are just the right height. Paint them with chalkboard paint and your Write Dance table is ready to use.

Paper

All types and sizes are suitable. Ask a printer for leftovers because Write Dance needs a lot of paper. Slippy paper is unsuitable. Rolls of wallpaper without relief or large sheets of drawing or painting paper can be used. We always Write Dance on large surfaces. If you don't have any of these at hand but you do have some plain A4 paper you can always draw or reinforce the movements on top of each other with colour crayons or pieces of chalk. After all, it is all about movement and not about producing a perfect shape or figure.

Sticky materials or masking tape

As both hands will be used, attach the sheets of paper to the table top or surface with sticky materials, for example, Blu-Tac, masking tape or plasticine. Plain sticky tape is not really suitable because it is difficult to remove from the tables afterwards.

A large sheet of plastic

This is perfect for doodling or scrimbling. A large piece of plastic can also be filled with a little water, provided it is held by some children and their teacher. Put a little bit of crepe paper in it and the water will colour while swaying it gently from side to side. If you add some bath foam, some paint and little balls or marbles, it will give you a wonderful display of colour.

12. Scrimbling Materials

Chalk
Plain chalkboard chalk is suitable, but do consider asthmatic children who react to chalk dust. Use as many colours as possible.

Old or short wax crayons
These are always suitable, while new and long pieces of crayon might break while using them, which could lead to unnecessary disappointment. Moreover old pieces of crayon can be gripped from the top, which is conducive to preparing children's hand position for when they are ready to do some real handwriting.

Chunky short markers
These are always popular with any child as the colours are bright, but wax crayons are more durable and it is the movements that count and not the results. It is always advisable to vary materials.

Plain pencils
These are not quite as suitable to be held in both hands as pre-school children can't grip them well in their little fists (not even if they are thick pencils). However, if they use a pencil only as a temporary alternative it is possible for them to copy the basic movements on top of each other, or to reinforce them.

Sponges
Cut a standard cleaning sponge into six to eight small pieces and place them in small trays with a little water. Dry cloths should always be available. Children who are not yet capable of holding pieces of chalk enjoy playing on the board with sponges. Squeezing sponges, drying the surface (with the basic movements) and wiping and stamping their feet all make for an enjoyable experience, regardless of the level of development of their motor skills.

Tip: Attach pegs to the sponges if it is not desirable to have wet hands. It is also possible to use little sticks (100mm – 120mm), wrapped in a piece of foam plastic, secured with fine wire for paint scrimbling.

Scrimbling and Write Dancing with sponges is an option too!

Cloths for cleaning up
Try making a print before using the cloths. We make one by spreading a sheet of A3 across the coloured slippery material, pressing it down slowly and then pulling the paper off. We can dry the print on the floor or on a washing line and then use it as a background for scrimbling with crayons. We could also fold the print and cut out a shape, such as a heart, an apple or a butterfly.

Remove most of the slippery material with paper tissues or kitchen roll. Now spray a very small amount of shaving foam and water on the surface and clean the table completely by scrimbling with flannels on both hands. Don't forget to use the top part of the cloths as well turning them over. Don't forget the edges of the tables!

Chunky brushes
The focus of the movements should be on gross motor skills. First allow the children to scrimble with their hands, next with their fingers, their fingertips and then, for example, with chunky brushes.

Cotton wool and cotton wool balls
These make a nice soft material to rub over your body or, if they are a little damp, to make prints on the table and on the board or on a plastic surface. Putting them into water and squeezing them can be fun too!

Shaving foam
This makes a perfect Write Dance material. It smells great and they can squiggle around in it, draw lines and dots, or anything you can imagine. Use a dropping pipette to introduce a water colour which makes wonderful effects. Keep it slippery with some bath foam or fill an empty shower spray with water and spray it over the bath foam now and again.

Bath foam
This can also be used for writing movements or scrimbling, or even to wash teddies (see Theme Play in Little Water Shute).

Finger paint
This makes a wonderful slippery material if it is mixed with wallpaper paste, salad oil or a lubricant. Try making some prints by laying a sheet of drawing paper over it and sliding your hands over the top to bring out the print as if by magic.

Sand
Sprinkle some sand on a tray with upright edges or make a sandpit or a sand table.

Finger dancing
This is something which we will only do with our fingers on the table top if there isn't any writing material readily available. If we can feel what it is like to work with dry and wet materials on the self-made board, then the feet can be used, too, which makes it very exciting.

Paper eye masks
Scrimbling with their eyes shut or wearing a mask stimulates sensory perception, sense of touch and free movement. Only do this if the child is ready for it. Many pre-school children might feel frightened when they can't see, while others might consider it a challenge. The surprise when they take off their masks and see what they have created on the writing surface always gives them a lot of pleasure and encourages their self-confidence. Playing with 'warm water masks' on their faces will have a similar effect.

13. Materials for Theme Play

Movements in their spaces:
• ribbons, scarves, streamers, garlands, strips of material, strips of paper or newspaper, confetti
• soft materials need to be put on a sheet, which can be held by a couple of children
• a big sheet of plastic to scrimble on or to put some water in with a piece of crepe paper.

On the floor:
• skittles, boxes, hoops, tracks drawn in chalk, ropes, and strips or snippets of paper or cloth.

14. The Role of the Teacher

Moving
The role of the adult is to offer the opportunity to make as many movements as possible, to offer enough space and material for experiments and to discover new things. It will be necessary to establish a certain routine before it is possible to think up variations together with the children. A routine opens up ways to free fantasies and fun, in their spaces, on their boards and on paper.

Reading out and telling stories
Once it's time to move on to a new theme, you need to begin with reading the story. The child will soon discover the freedom to add their own experiences, which encourages the power of their imagination and creativity. It is possible to present the stories and songs in succession according to the alternatives within 'Home' and 'Funfair', but it is also possible to combine and alternate, depending on special days, events, holidays or seasons.

Sitting and standing
In order to achieve a smooth transition from the well-known reading of a familiar story to unfamiliar 'movements', the teacher should begin with demonstrating the movements sitting down without the music, but with appropriate sounds or noises, after having read the story and listened to all the tales. The children will then copy the movements while seated. Next the movements can be repeated while standing. The children will be eager to join in of their own accord. Moving their bodies comes naturally to all children.

Should I join in?
If one child refuses to join for a considerable time, it might be because they are already demonstrating difficulties with gross motor skills and they need to be observed. It could mean that they find it difficult to express their emotions in a physical way. Such a child has 'frozen' and might need special help and assistance to begin to move naturally again.

Scrimbling

The teacher will need to demonstrate and join in during the transition from moving in their spaces to scrimbling. Adults need to watch that there is a balance between scrimbling (or repeated movements) and plain drawing. Children learn from their parents or older siblings how they can draw dolls, figures, shapes and letters. They will proudly want to show their teacher what they can do. It has been like that since the introduction of compulsory education. However, in our age of technology with insufficient links between gross and fine motor skill movements, experiences and emotions, Write Dance in the Early Years and its invaluable scrimbling can be a means to preparing a pre-school child's sensorimotor and psychomotor skills for infant activties.

Write Dance

We hope that Write Dance in the Early Years will be continued and possibly combined with Write Dance, so that when children begin to learn to write letters and use joined up handwriting, they are completely ready. Moreover, we would like them to enjoy what they do and produce smooth, flowing and springy first sentences and a flow of words on paper. When pre-school children or infants begin to make their own combinations of movements and Write Dance in their own games and drawings, we can assume that the preparatory writing signs have been well stored in their brain programme. The teacher does not need to force or impose anything. It would only have a contrary effect and Write Dancing would not achieve its goal.

Pieces of chalk

It is not unusual for a pre-school child to take hold of pieces of chalk initially in a palmer or fist grip. This is when the wrists are vertical and the fingers are gripping the pieces of chalk like you would grip a hammer. Hand and wrist exercises in their spaces, finger dancing on the table, scrimbling in shaving cream and bath foam and finger paint will loosen up the child's wrists, meaning they will also be able to grip the pieces of chalk from the top, which is beneficial to writing at a later stage.

By picking up the pieces of chalk from above, the wrist will take on the correct writing posture. It is right to offer some corrections now and then to do scrimbling on paper, though without too much pressure.

The board

If a child does not respond, or if they find it annoying because their wrists are still too stiff, the board and the accompanying sponges and cloths are a suitable means to work with wet and dry materials. Pressing down on pieces of chalk when they get wet makes a lovely mess and could be continued in shaving foam, bath foam, water, sand and wet clay. All this helps to loosen up the wrists.

Tip: Any paper Write Dance works of art made by the children which they don't wish to take with them and they are finished with, can be folded by the teacher and cut into shapes such as a butterfly, a heart, or an apple. Thus the child sees that a shape is hidden in their actions. They could also be used as a background for handicrafts and three-dimensional art works.

Illustrations

The illustrations in this book are very simple, which makes them easy to copy and they can be used as a source of inspiration. If necessary they can be enlarged, coloured and pasted onto something so that the children can scrimble around them.

15. A Working Method in Ten Steps for Write Dance in the Early Years

1. Stick down sensory or scrimble materials beforehand and fasten down the paper with Blu-Tac or masking tape. Provide sufficient wet sponges and dry cloths.

2. Read out the story several times.

3. Allow the children to tell their own stories.

4. Demonstrate movements with sounds and noises.

5. Ask the children to copy them.

6. Sing accompanied or unaccompanied by the CD.

7. Perform actions accompanied by music.

8. Continue actions accompanied by instrumental music.

9. Scrimble and/or work with sensory materials or play games and repeat songs with actions.

10. Repeat scrimbling.

This working method develops gradually and some points are repeated several times before progressing to the next point. Allow plenty of time, days if necessary. After all, very young children can only keep their attention to an assignment for 15 to 20 minutes and repetition creates confidence, pleasure and a feeling of safety.

	Home		Funfair
Home 1	Sandy Hill	Funfair 1	Watermill
Home 2	Kringeli-Krangeli	Funfair 2	My Dinky Car
Home 3	Pat-a-cake	Funfair 3	Merry-go-round
Home 4	The Staircase	Funfair 4	The Procession
Home 5	The Toy Train	Funfair 5	Air Train
Home 6	Tickle Tree	Funfair 6	Tree & Fairy Lights
Home 7	Little Water Shute	Funfair 7	Big Water Shute
Home 8	The Rainbow	Funfair 8	The Gateway
Home 9	Little Sun	Funfair 9	Dear Sun, Dear Moon
Home 10	Straight, Bent, Cross, Happy		

Scrimbling and sensory experience	Write Dance (4-8)
Straight 'ship' or rocking movements - upwards and downwards or swaying *Experience wet or dry play with sand and water*	1. Volcano
Swinging movements and lines *Finding or losing their way, or finding their bearings and making their way home*	2. Countryside Walk / Krongelidong Animals
Circular movements, continuous tune *Fat, full, bloated, dizzy*	3. Circles and Eights
Angular movements, rhythm and counting *High, low, in a line and regularity*	4. Robot
Looped movements upwards and downwards, quickly and slowly *Quickly and slowly, down on the floor and up above*	5. Train
Random and focused (grabbing) movements *Standing firmly on the ground with movements freely in the air or in their spaces*	6. Tree
Swaying movements *Water, agility, calm or rough, high and low*	7. The Sea / Silver Wings
Arched movements *Arches, standing up, safety and protection*	8. Cats /
Circular and straight movements starting from a fixed or central point *Hot and cold, summer and winter, nearby and far away, 'me and you'*	9. Mandala / Bloemenkrans
Straight and circular, set and free movements *Security, flexibility, adjustment, feelings and emotions*	

Yoyo and Meema are going to the beach with their Mum. They both have their buckets and spades. Meema has a red spade and a blue bucket, Yoyo has a green spade and a yellow bucket.

'Look, there's the sea,' says Meema. 'Are you going in with me, Yoyo?' They both run into the water. Crash! Yoyo trips and is soaking wet. Meema and Mum have to laugh. 'Fortunately you were wearing your swimming trunks,' said Mum. Quickly Yoyo takes off his t-shirt and trousers and begins to roll in the waves.

'Don't go any further, Yoyo,' says Mum. But of course Yoyo already knows.

'Come on, Yoyo, we will make a high sand hill,' says Meema and starts digging with her red spade. Yoyo gets out of the water and picks up his green spade.

'I will make my hill here,' he says. It is a warm day, so Yoyo dries quickly.

'Your hill is much bigger than mine, Yoyo,' says Meema, 'will you come and help me?'

Yoyo, a strong boy, immediately throws a big spade full of sand on Meema's hill. Then they fill Yoyo's buckets with water and they use Mum's hairbrush to make rain over their sand hills. They dip the brush in water and give it a good shake.

'Now it is raining heavily,' says Meema. She has found another brush in her beachbag and beats both brushes together creating big drops on her sand hill. They press down the sand of their hills with their feet and begin to dig burrows.

'Wobble, wobble, wobble,' says Meema and Yoyo joins in. And then she suddenly discovers she has covered her little blue bucket with sand.

Song

My hill is high, so very hi-igh,
Your hill is high, so very hi-igh.
I'm tumbling down, look here,
Wobble, wobble, wobble…
Oh dear!

Here comes a cloud, a big big clou-oud,
Here comes a cloud, a big big clou-oud.
It's raining on my hill,
Tippy, tappy, tat,
I'm wet!

Words	Movements
On the beach - lots of sa-and On the beach - lots of sa-and	*Wave your arms in front of you from side to side or pretend you are shovelling a small heap of sand*
My hill is here	*Make downward movements with your arms on one side of your body and bend your knees deeply*
Your hill is there	*Repeat: now on the other side of your body*
They make a fine pair	*Turn your wrists upward and open your hands*
My hill is high, so very hi-igh	*Stand on tiptoes and stretch up high with your arms*
Your hill is high, so very hi-igh	*Twist both arms in the air towards another child*
I'm tumbling down, look here	*Lower your arms and bend your knees deeply*
Wobble, wobble, wobble...	*Dig like a dog*
Oh dear!	*Spread your arms in the air*
Here comes a cloud, a big big clou-oud Here comes a cloud, a big big clou-oud	*Bend your arms as if you are embracing a big teddy bear*
It's raining on my hill	*Shake your hands*
Tippy, tappy, tat	*Shake your hands quicker*
I'm wet!	*Shake the 'wet' off your hands and bend your knees*

Scrimbling	Illustrations
Standing or sitting: draw horizontal lines with a piece of chalk in both hands	
Draw lines downward on one side of the surface (it is a little hill)	
Draw lines downward on the other side	
Twist your wrists upward with the pieces of chalk in your hands	
Draw lines upward on one side, above the first hill	
Draw lines upward on the other side	
Draw wavy lines downward	
Dashes up and down	
Arms up in the air with pieces of chalk in your hands	
Circling around	
Draw dashes from your wrists	
Stipple everywhere	
Powerful lines downward	

Expressions on the scrimbling surface

Foundation movement: movements from side to side, and up and down

In this first song, toddlers and infants will experience the connection between
expressions in the air and the same expressions on the scrimbling surface.
'The hill is high' is expressed by drawing lines upward, and the cloud by
circling around. That is how the scrimbling surface becomes a 'country of discovery'
in which each child expresses his or herself in their own way, while becoming aware
of the contrasts between horizontal and vertical, upward and downward, round and
straight movements, etc.
If the children are still finding it difficult to follow the movements precisely and to
alternate, first practise the movements individually. It is not necessary to switch on
the music immediately. In due course, when the child begins to feel more at ease
scrimbling and the music becomes familiar, the foundation movements will become
more and more fluid. Try using wet sensory materials while scrimbling!

Theme Play

• One or more children are kneeling down on the floor. Their heads are tucked away between their arms. They are sandy hills. We will play Drop the Handkerchief with older pre-school children and infants and when the music has finished there will be a small spade or toy lying behind a child. We can leave out the running away depending on the group.

• The teacher draws a variety of circles or spots on the floor, or alternatively we can use hoops. Each child sits down in her hoop or circle, her 'sandy hill', and repeats the actions in the way she chooses.

• The teacher gives a toy or object to one of the children. The child hides it under his clothes. Nobody knows where it is. The actions are carried out freely or as the child perceives them according to the music. During the last notes the child will show his object as a surprise.

• Hiding something can be related to the seasons, for example, in autumn we can hide something under a pile of leaves. Before Christmas we could decorate stockings. We stuff them with other objects and newspaper snippets. The actual present is hidden at the bottom.

• We make a real sand hill in the sand pit outside or in the classroom, and heap more and more sand on it while singing or making noises. Finally we sprinkle water over the hill from two wet brushes, imitating rain. If we have hidden an object we can dig for it while singing or saying 'wobble wobble'. Repetition might encourage the children to sing the other words of the song spontaneously.

• We could also make a hill from clay or sweet sticky pudding rice in which we have hidden a couple of raisins. Otherwise we could cover an object in a couple of layers of plaster and when it has hardened we can paint our pieces of art.

Story   *Matching Theme Funfair: My Dinky Car*

Yoyo and Meema have spent the whole day playing on the beach. Now they are on their way home. They shake the sand off their bare bodies and get dressed. They are very tired and their tiny feet find it so difficult walking through the warm sand.

Finally they are on the footpath home. This is much better. Mum, Yoyo and Meema sing the song 'Kringeli-krangeli krongelidong' each time they see a long bend. They walk in a straight line and then from side to side. They like that game and they forget their tiredness after a full day on the beach. Suddenly Meema stops.

'Mum, there is so much sand in my shoe, what shall I do?'

'Shake it,' says Mum, and Meema gives it a good shake. The sand pours out from the toes and her heel.

'It's a good job you are wearing sandals, Meema,' says Yoyo, 'otherwise you would have had to take off your shoes.'

'I can see our house,' says Mum, but they still have quite a way to go. And because the three of them keep singing it seems to go quicker and suddenly they find they are home again. And who sits down on the pavement?

Song

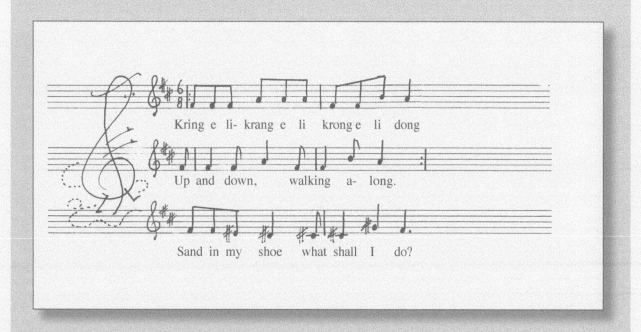

Kringeli krangeli krongelidong
Up and down, walking a-long
Sand in my shoe what shall I do?
Sand in my shoe what shall I do?
Wobble, wobble, wobble...
Go sand!
Kringeli - krangeli krongelidong
Far from home and on we roam
A long long way to go
And then we'll be back home (4x)

KRINGELI-KRANGELI 2   Home CD no. 3 - instr. 4

Words	Movements
Kringeli krangeli krongelidong Up and down, walking along	*Make krongelidong wriggles with hands and wrists and your whole body*
Kringeli krangeli krongelidong Up and down, walking along	*Continue krongelidong wriggles*
Sand in my shoe what shall I do? Sand in my shoe what shall I do?	*Stamp your feet*
Wobble, wobble, wobble...	*Dig like dogs and stamp your feet*
Go sand!	*Stretch your arms in front of you*
Kringeli krangeli krongelidong	*Krongelidong wriggles*
Far from home and on we roam	*Move arms from side to side in a relaxed manner*
Kringeli krangeli krongelidong	*Krongelidong wriggles*
Far from home and on we roam	*Move arms from side to side in a relaxed manner*
A long long way to go A long long way to go	*Take big steps down the classroom or in the yard* *Sitting: stamp your feet on the ground*
And then we'll be back home (4x)	*Jump up and down in your place*

Scrimbling	Illustrations
Round and meandering looped movements in all directions	
Continue with round and meandering looped movements	
Dashes up and down	
Continue with dashes up and down	
Big lines upward	
Draw meandering loops	
Horizontal lines from side to side	
Meandering loops	
Horizontal lines from side to side	
Draw long lines	
Jump and stipple	

Expressions on the scrimbling surface

Foundation movement: *meandering movements and looped lines*

Wriggles, krongeli wriggles, or krongelidong (wriggles) are typical Write Dance words. They always mean the same: arch and bend using all the joints in your body: fingers, wrists, elbows, hips, knees and ankles. On the scrimbling surface they become meandering loops in any direction. We might do this again with sensory material, or with crayons on a board or on paper. The meandering movements help the child manage the many changes of direction from which handwriting emerges. By first sensing these wriggly movements in their own bodies the child becomes aware of the challenging possibilities on the scrimbling surface. Some children will respond immediately with gusto, while other children move quite cautiously and will for instance only play with a small part of the surface, only draw thin lines, or only use one finger in shaving foam or slippery paint.

Most letters and join-ups consist of round and rounded writing movements. Many children find it difficult; they are tense and move around curves with difficulty and in an angular fashion. The more supple a child's body is at an early age, the more naturally the child will cope with all the movements on the writing surface, following each other at a rapid pace. In *Write Dance in the Early Years* the experimentation with letter shapes is not as important as the preparatory movements in which music plays a part.

Krongelidong wriggles are healthy and make your letters nice and round!

Theme Play

• Take a piece of chalk and draw a wriggly, bendy 'krongli-dong' path across the room or in the playground and let the children follow it.

• Twisting and turning like the krongelidong means twisting and turning in the air or on the ground like a krongelidong animal. A krongelidong animal is an animal we will frequently meet in Write Dance. You can make one out of circular movements and loops: eyes, ears, whiskers and paws, and hey presto! First you twist and turn like the krongelidong with your entire body, lying down or standing up, and then on the writing surface. In the sand you can also twist and turn with your fingers, making tracks and then drawing eyes with your index finger.

• A child or a cuddly toy lies on a sheet or blanket and other children pull it along twisting and turning in different directions through the hall.

• Cut out pictures and stick them onto a big sheet of paper. Use a writing implement or simply your fingers to wriggle round them to the music along a bendy road. We continue to use different colours over each other. Don't trace but consolidate the shape in your own personal swing and style (see the Introduction for a reminder of consolidating).

• The children bring their cuddly toys from home. Spread them around in a large area. Listening to the music we weave our way round them. When the music stops each child tries to find his own cuddly animal. The children will also wriggle their own animal in the air, far away, close to them, high up in the air or just above the ground.

• As we did in Sandy Hill we can sit down in a hoop, this time with our cuddly animals. It's our little den. When the music begins to play we get up and weave our way around like the krongelidong.

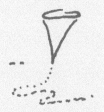

• Fill your shoes with sand in the sandpit and let it all run out again. There is another option, which is to fold a paper cone, filling it with very fine sand and then cutting off a tiny tip, just like a piping bag. We can use it to make twisty tracks on a tray or on the self-made board. This technique can be applied to all the following themes to make straight lines, waves, circles and semi-circles, arches and boats.

Story

Matching Theme Funfair: Merry-go-round

'Today we will make something easy for lunch,' says Mum, 'how about making a pat-a-cake? Come, let's make the pastry.'

Mum puts butter, flour, eggs and milk in a bowl and Yoyo and Meema take turns stirring with the wooden spoon.

When it is Meema's turn, she sings, 'Stir well, round and round,' but Yoyo won't join in. He tries to get rid of all the lumps by squeezing them with his spoon, but it doesn't always work.

Mum gives him the mixer. 'Tap-tap-tap-tap,' says the mixer hitting the bowl.

And the pastry is ready. Now they've got to grease the baking tin. Yoyo's butter slips on the floor. Meema is more careful and finishes the job. She has done it very nicely, without making a mess. Clever Meema.

Yoyo is very hungry and can't wait, so he takes a big spoonful out of the tin. Mum is very cross. Meema and Yoyo go to play while the cake is in the oven. After an hour they come back to taste the cake.

Meema gives a piece of cake to her two favourite dolls - she pretends they are siblings.

'I have eaten a third piece,' says Yoyo, but Meema has left hers, because she is no longer hungry and prefers to play.

'And now off to bed,' says Mum. But Yoyo and Meema don't feel tired. Dad plays a game with them on the stairs: one-and-two-and-three…!

Song

Stir well, round and round,

The pastry makes a gurgling sound.

Milk and eggs and a very good beat,

A pat - a - cake is nice and sweet.

> Stir well, round and round,
> One for my mum and one for my gran.
> Yum yum yum and tum tum tum,
> My pat-a-cake is down in my tum.

Words	Movement
Stir well, round and round The pastry makes a gurgling sound	*Make stirring movements with your hands and your whole body*
Milk and eggs and a very good beat	*Clench your fists up in the air, 'grabbing' movements*
A pat- a- cake is nice and sweet	*Draw circles on your tummy*
Stir well, round and round	*Stirring movement*
One for my mum and one for my gran	*Point towards another child (mum), then to another (gran)*
Yum yum yum and tum tum tum My pat-a-cake is down in my tum	*Pretend you are eating the pat-a-cake finally drawing circles on your tummy*

Scrimbling	Illustrations
Draw two circles in the same or in the opposite direction	
Stipple to the rhythm	
Scrimbling around	
Scrimbling around	
Place two pieces of chalk first in one circle, then in the other	
Scrimble around and stipple in the centre to 'down in my tum'	

Expressions on the scrimbling surface

Foundation movement: rotating or circular movements

It is easier to draw straight lines than circular lines. Boys sometimes find it more difficult to make circular movements. Circular lines 'fill' feelings and emotions, straight lines ignore them and are more cerebral. In general the motor skills of girls develop more quickly than those of boys; boys prefer to ignore the complex and emotional pattern of signals and prefer to be purpose-minded. Therefore it is very important for boys to begin making circular movements at an early age. They can do so by clasping their hands together and following that particular movement through, or making individual circular movements with their hands apart.

Writing letters and join-ups is achieved by letting circular and straight lines flow into each other, without having to think. It should become an automatic process, without hesitation, and without jagged or slipping lines. Occasionally, alternate the circular themes such as Pat-a-Cake and Merry-Go-Round with themes such as The Staircase and The Procession. If you have not learnt to sense circular movements in your body and on the scrimbling surface, you will continue to move stiffly and awkwardly. A circular movement relaxes, a straight movement tenses. If you increase your awareness of the cooperation between fingers, head and heart at an early stage it will give you flexibility in the way you function overall. Your handwriting reflects it.

Theme Play

• The children stir within a hoop, and then lie down in or on the hoop and turn round and round as if they were a cake in a tin.

• Spray enough shaving cream on a big piece of plastic, or directly on the table, to enable you to make a cake with round movements. The children are given a wet cloth and grease the tin by swirling the cloth to the left and to the right.

• Make circular or rounded movements with different parts of the body: hands, arms, legs, head, stomach... while sitting or lying down. In winter we could imagine making snowballs. We pretend to be snowballs by rolling about in the classroom or making the snowballs out of little balls of paper.

• Draw a circle on the floor with a piece of chalk and walk on the line with the children following you. Ask the children to erase the line with a brush or another cleaning instrument.

• Walking, twisting or dancing in the classroom: when the music is paused, all the children stand in the circle; when the music plays again, they disperse.

• Making pastry for a cake: the children stir in turns while singing the song. Baking real cakes could be another activity!

'Come on Yoyo and Meema, let's go, off to bed,' says Dad. 'Do you know what we will do? We will count the steps. How many steps are there Meema?' Meema doesn't know.

Dad shows her what to do. He sets one foot on the first step and counts out loud. Yoyo and Meema follow him.

'One,' says Dad.

'Two,' says Yoyo.

'Three,' says Meema.

'Four,' says Mum, standing at the bottom of the stairs. And suddenly Pippa the cat runs upstairs taking big leaps.

'She has forgotten to count,' exclaims Dad. But cats can't count anyway, or do you think they can?

'I don't want to go to bed yet,' says Meema and she quickly runs down all the steps. Yoyo copies her.

'Alright, you can play, but just for a bit. Is that okay Mum?' Dad asks. She says it's fine and they have a really good time. Meema takes a big leap when she reaches the bottom step.

'I can take two in one go,' says Meema and she shows them.

'And I can take three,' says Dad and the three of them get very excited.

'Now you should really go to bed,' Mum shouts from the kitchen, and they count the remaining steps.

Seven, eight and nine and ten, one final jump and Yoyo is back up again.

'Did you see that jump, Dad?'

'Yes and it was a clever one,' says Dad, 'and now off to bed and then we will sing the song once more.'

Song

One and two and three and four and five and six and seven,
Wait a little minute,
Wait a little minute,
I haven't moved an inch,
A teeny weenie pinch,
Seven eight and nine and ten,
I can jump…
As high as great Big Ben! (4x)

Words	Movements
One and two and three and four and five and six and seven	*Pretend you are walking up the stairs*
Wait a li- ttle min- ute Wait a li- ttle min- ute	*Stop*
It's not my bed- time yet I'm fly- ing in a jet	*Shake your head slowly*
Seven eight and nine and ten	*Climbing stairs*
I can jump…	*A big leap up and down or forward. Sitting: Raise your feet and let them descend*
As high as great Big Ben! (4x)	*Jump up and down without moving forward*
One and two and three and four and five and six and seven	*Climbing stairs*
Wait a li- ttle min- ute Wait a li- ttle min- ute	*Stop*
I haven't moved an inch A teeny weenie pinch	*Stop dead with your arms straight along your body*
Seven eight and nine and ten	*Climbing stairs, lift your feet higher*
I can jump…	*Big leap up and down or forward Sitting: Raise your feet and let them descend*
As high as great Big Ben! (4x)	*Jump up and down and keep your arms up*

Scrimbling	Illustrations
Form right angles	
Hold pieces of chalk in the air and wait	
Draw lines from side to side and simultaneously shake your head slowly	
Form right angles	
Draw a big arch	
Draw lines upward	
Draw right angles	
Hold pieces of chalk in the air and wait	
Place hands on the surface and keep them still	
Form right angles from the surface upward	
Draw a big arch	
Lines upward	

Expressions on the scrimbling surface

Foundation movement: **straight and jagged movements, lines and shapes**

It is easier for a child to draw jagged lines than round ones as the simplest path between two dots is a straight line. Very often it is given too much force, especially when it is only one line. By first repeatedly tracing straight lines over each other to and fro, we are giving the right impulse to start up motor skills. This is how straight lines are programmed spontaneously. Performing tasks with right angles can then be carried out without being tense and without overusing force and energy. Considerable will power is used to interrupt a long line by a right angle, which might be easier for boys than for girls. Marching in time will control physical coordination; moreover it contrasts with the melody which gives freedom for personal interpretations. Upright or vertical lines move towards or away from the body. Flat lines move backwards and forwards, from left to right. When vertical and flat lines cross each other, they automatically create jagged figures which we can trace with our fingers. Finger dancing! We count aloud and sense the difference between arches and loops. It can be a good idea to alternate the straight themes in The Staircase and Procession with the rounded themes in Pat-a-cake and Merry-Go-Round within one lesson and on the same surface. The quick alternation of round and straight movements will eventually improve the dexterity and flexibility of handwriting.

Theme Play

• The teacher beats a drum slowly and the children take big slow steps. We can imagine ourselves going upstairs. Can we count slowly while we are doing it? Next we take a big jump or a very small one: variation creates suppleness in body, mind and on the writing surface.

• A fast beat on the drum: the children walk quickly (running up and down the stairs).
The drum stops: the children stop dead (stopping halfway up the stairs). Alternate a couple of times. We could also attach bells to their feet to reinforce the movements.

• Draw big and small lines; we take a big stride when we see a big line and a small step when we come to a small line.

* Can we walk step by step, inch by inch?

* Now big jumps and little jumps!

• A staircase is angular; look for angular objects or name some angular objects. Make a game with sharp and round objects. The children sit down in a circle with a round sheet over their laps. Unfamiliar round objects are passed round and named. We will do the same with a sheet held tight and angular objects.

Matching Theme Funfair: Air Train

It is Yoyo's birthday and he has been given a wooden train. It is a beautiful train, the carriages are red and the engine has yellow lines along the side.

'This train has travelled all the way from toy land,' Grandpa said when Yoyo unpacked the present.

Meema and Yoyo play with the train and its five carriages. The doors can open and close. It isn't difficult to assemble the tracks. Yoyo and Meema have laid them in a nice circle. It means the train can continue to run round and round. It runs smoothly over the track. Meema likes the gentle sound when Yoyo pushes it along carefully.

'I wouldn't mind being that train myself,' says Meema. 'I would carry everybody wherever they want to go across the world.'

Yoyo stops and suddenly shouts:

'Now we are at a station, please get off the train.'

'What's the name of the station?' asks Meema, but Yoyo doesn't know, he is too busy opening and closing the doors. Meema thinks of a cute name, can you imagine which one?

Song

Puffa, puffa, puffa, puffa, puffa train,
Just look here, I am a train.
Puffa, puffa, puffa, puffa, puffa train,
Here we're going through the rain.
Just a mo,
Rightee-ho!
We are ready, off we go.

Words	Movements
Puff- a, puff- a, puff- a, puff- a, puff-a train Just look here, I am a train	*Move your arms round in parallel against the body like an old-fashioned train and follow each other in a line*
Puff- a, puff- a, puff- a, puff- a, puff-a train Just look here, I am a train	*Train movements or 'loops of smoke'*
All get on	*One step forward*
Off she goes	*Moving further forward*
Toot toot, the whistle blows	*Pull an imaginary whistle with one hand*
Puff- a, puff- a, puff- a, puff- a, puff-a train, Just look here, I am a train	*Train movements or 'loops of smoke'*
Puff- a, puff- a, puff- a, puff- a, puff-a train, Here we're going through the rain	*Train movements or 'loops of smoke'*
Just a mo Rightee-ho!	*Stop where you are and put your arms down*
We are ready, off we go	*Walking forward*

Scrimbling	Illustrations
Circling around and making loops walk, with one or both hands	
Circling around and making loops walk, with one or both hands	
Placing a hand or hands in the circles	
Walking loops moving upward	
Lines downward	
Scrimbling around and making loops walk	
Scrimbling around and making loops walk	
Placing hands together on the writing surface	
Walking loops upward	

Expressions on the scrimbling surface

Foundation movement: round movements moving along in the air and thus becoming loops

In this train song we form circles with our elbows tight against our bodies. That is how we imitate an old-fashioned locomotive. We could also mimic the smoke with our arms in front of us by making loops which move either towards or away from each other. The loops are created on the scrimbling area if we make the circles 'walk'. The loops might follow the bendy lines. But the loops of smoke might just as well fill the entire scrimbling surface. Or even circle up into the air from the surface. The loops could move downward or upward, in or out. The advanced scrimbler could even reinforce these movements with different colours.

A fun scrimbling exercise is to let the train leave and then to move faster and faster. Of course we add the appropriate sounds, 'choo choo choo' or 'sh sh sh'... The train may move forward and backward. It is also possible to have the train travel along the edges which frame the surface.

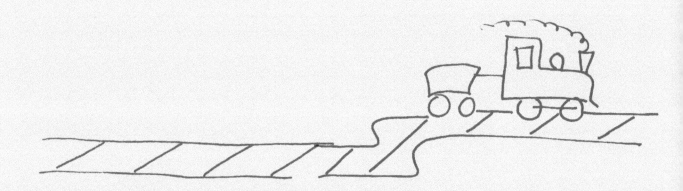

Theme Play

• Follow each other through the classroom like a train, swinging the arms forward in line with each other and backward in a similar fashion. It is also possible to take a piece of chalk and draw a train track on the floor. We can make some marks with confetti, snippets of paper or by spreading sand. We travel through the field of marks in our train. It is also possible to express this on a writing surface. If something is knocked over by accident and makes a mark, we could in future pass by in the 'cloth or mark train' to tidy up the 'marked area', if you like while singing the song.

• Sitting down on the floor or on a long bench continue to swing the arms round in line with each other or casually above your head. Set the music to pause. The arms have stopped moving, the music continues and the arms turn backward. We can also do this while walking.

• Pretend to be a train by lining up chairs behind each other.

• Move arms horizontally away from each other and towards each other, like smoke or make the movement of turning wheels. Both hands and wrists make looped movements. We reinforce the actions with ribbons, scarves or strips of crepe paper.

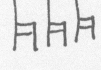

• We sit down on the floor with our legs stretched forward.

Puffa puffa	The arms turn
All get on	Open legs
Off she goes	Close legs
Toot toot, the whistle blows	Draw knees up to stomach

• Place small items in a line on the floor, first walk around them in loops and then allow the children to draw on the floor with chalk.

Upward (garlands)
or downward (arches)

Inward (hollow)   or outward (rounded)

The song is sung by the teacher and the children with or without the CD; alternatively we first make some noises to get the feel of the movements and learn to alternate them.

Story   *Matching Theme Funfair: Tree & Fairy Lights*

Autumn has arrived in Yoyo's and Meema's garden. Dad has swept up a whole pile of leaves. There are acorns all over the ground and Meema fetches a bucket for them. Yoyo gets his little rake and rakes more leaves towards the big pile. The leaves fly in all directions and Yoyo throws himself onto the big heap. He takes off his coat and the leaves tickle him everywhere, on his neck, in his hair, between his fingers, on his legs, everywhere. He really enjoys rolling around and he has almost flattened the pile of leaves. Meema's bucket is nearly full. She only picks up acorns with little caps and leaves the others. Then she begins to roll in the leaves, but keeps her jacket on so that the leaves can't tickle her. Yoyo invents a funny little game.

'You know what, Meema, I will throw up the leaves and you've got to catch them, okay?'
He takes a big lump of leaves in both hands. Meema grabs in all directions. It isn't easy at all. Her hands try to catch.

'I've got a chestnut,' she cries out with delight. It is a beauty and so shiny. She puts it in her pocket. The rain begins to fall gently, so they go indoors. What will they be playing?

Song

Leaves and leaves they tickle

Hands and fin- gers pri- ckle,

Snatch it, look here, snatch

Watch it, try and catch.

Watch the acorns tumble,
Acorns they roll and rumble,
Snatch it, look here, snatch,
Watch it, try and catch.

Words	Movements
Leaves and leaves they tickle Hands and fin- gers pri- ckle	*Shaking your whole body and waggling hands and fingers*
Snatch it, look here, snatch	*Stretching both arms in turn and making grabbing movements*
Watch it, try and catch	*Continue grabbing movements*
Watch the acorns tumble	*Stretching your arms in front of you and dropping them*
Acorns they roll and rumble	*Dropping your arms even lower and bending your knees deeply* *Sitting: dropping your arms and resting your head in your lap*
Snatch it, look here, snatch Watch it, try and catch	*Stretching your arms, making gripping and grabbing movements*

Scrimbling	Illustrations
Drawing krongelidong wriggles and squiggles	
Drawing long lines	
Stipple to the rhythm	
Draw wavy lines down	
Lines downward	
Draw long lines first and then stipple	

Expressions on the scrimbling surface

Foundation movement: squiggles, dots and lines

This song is all about switching between relaxing and tensing, random shaking and focused grabbing and gripping. We know from ourselves and see in children that it is not always easy to give your whole body a good shake.

And that is exactly what we need to relearn. Quick movements from side to side will make our hands, arms, shoulders, head and legs tremble. We squealed with delight when we were little babies and were raised into the air and given a gentle shake. This fun might return by means of the Tickle Tree song. The wind shakes all our branches and leaves.

If we hold our shaking hands on the scrimbling surface, it will create automatic squiggles in all directions. Immediately after, we will express the grabbing movement in lines or dots to the rhythm of the music. The changes in the music are so obvious that the coordination of ears, eyes and hands is stimulated.

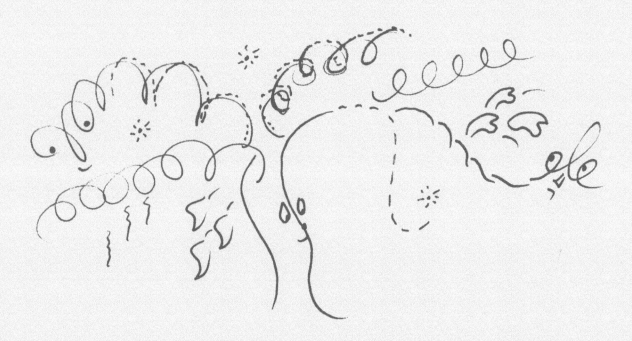

Theme Play

• Tickle your own body or somebody else's, with fingers, finger puppets, combs or anything you can think of. Alternate that with rubbing faces, arms and feet with cotton wool to sense the soft feeling in contrast. Or… go and tickle the teacher, all of you!

• Make a pile of leaves in autumn to play in. We could also put some crisps or soft biscuits in a plastic bag and crumble them entirely. Spread the crumbs out on a big cloth, take a straw and blow them together in a big heap.

• Move hands and fingers in shaving foam and scrimble. Use a pipette to add coloured drops. They could represent acorns in need of a wash.

• Make snatching movements while blindfolded or under a sheet to encourage the feeling sensation: pick chestnuts, acorns, branches and strong leaves out of a basket, name them and put them on the table.

• The teacher and the children discuss trees and woods. How do trees stand, straight or perpendicular, close or far apart, against a wall or in a big field? Children think of varieties and depict them. In this way we experience big and small, low and high, thick and thin, earth and sky. What do trees need in order to grow, what do trees look like in winter and in summer? Roll chestnuts and other autumn products on a sheet or cloth and 'play' with them by moving the cloth up and down. Stop the chestnuts and let them rest, they are tired of playing.

Matching Theme Funfair: Big Water Shute

Yoyo and Meema assemble their plastic slide in the bathroom. There are very many big and small pieces to make the slide into a real rolling shute. It is not an easy job but Yoyo knows exactly what to do and has a serious look on his face. The water shute is ready.

'Is it in the right position Meema?' he asks, and moves it a little more towards the centre of the table. The bottom part of the shute is now hanging over the edge of the bath. Meema has filled the bath with a bit of water and picks up her bucket full of acorns. She draws faces on them.

'The little acorn men can really swim,' she says. In a blue bucket she pours lots of water over the slide and she lets the acorn men tumble down one after the other. When they fall on the floor off the slide it makes them laugh. There are also acorns that do land in the bath and Meema makes high waves with her hands. They all continue to float but they lose their faces. Mum comes upstairs and sees the bathroom.

'It looks like a real swimming pool,' she says. The whole floor is wet. They dry everything up with towels and Mum says the slide can stay up until the following day.

Song

Hum-e- ty dump-e- ty bump-e- ty bump,

Little man tripped over the hump,

Dipp-e- ty dopp-e- ty dipp-e- ty day,

The acorn has turned its head away.

Tickety tackety tickety tack,
The little man's lying on his back,
Bippety boppety bippety ben,
The acorn has turned round again.

Words	Movements
Hump- e- ty dump- e- ty bump- e- ty bump	*Wavy movements with arms up in the air and sitting or standing and swaying from side to side*
Little man tripped over the hump	*Bend your head and stroke it in circular movements*
Dipp- e- ty dopp- e- ty dipp- e- ty day	*Wavy movement with your arms and sway, turn up your wrists to 'ty day'*
The acorn has turned its head away	*Turn your head slowly from side to side*
Tickety tackety tickety tack	*Wave your arms and/or sway your whole body* *Sit down on 'tack'*
The little man's lying on his back	*Lie on your back and roll from side to side*
Bippety boppety bippety ben	*Continue to roll from side to side*
The acorn has turned round again	*Continue to roll*

Scrimbling	Illustrations
Waves from side to side	
Circling around	
Waves from side to side, turn your wrists to 'ty day' (holding pieces of chalk in your hands)	
Draw lines from side to side	
Waves from side to side, turn wrists to 'tack'	
Make new waves	
Waves from side to side	
Draw lines from side to side	

Expressions on the scrimbling surface

Foundation movement: wavy movements from side to side and up and down

Wavy movements and lines arise from semi-circles where 'rounded' and 'hollow' semi-circles continue to alternate. If we are referring to horizontal wave movements, we could also call the rounded parts 'arches' and the hollow parts 'boats'. In order to make high and deep waves, we will first draw a line of circles which we will then follow, either over and under, or inside and outside. The circles are stones in the river or shells in the sea. When we draw a flat wave, we accompany ourselves aloud: 'and over and under, and over and under...' And when we make an upright wave, we say 'and out and in, and out and in...'

Of course we could also send paper boats sailing over the waves, while we sing a song such as 'Row, row, row the boat, gently down the stream'. Only afterwards do we turn on the music.

In the upright waves we recognize the letter s, but rather than starting on letters too soon, it is preferable to create chains by repeating the wavy movement along the circles to and fro.

Creating waves is good for general flexibility and to allow complicated movements to flow into each other. If this works well, jagged 'waves' and 'waves' only consisting of arches will not be as prominent!

Theme Play

• Place building bricks or boxes behind each other with approximately one metre between them. Hold a hose or a rope together with the children and weave in and out between the objects. Next all the children weave through in turn or in pairs. The end of the rope may drag over the ground so that the other children can see how to create a wavy movement.

• While walking along we spread our arms out like wings and occasionally bend our knees to fly 'high' and 'low'. We can imagine we are flying birds, snakes, dragons or horses. The more imagination, the better!

• Just relax lying on the floor listening to the sounds or move along crawling like waves.

• A couple of children hold a plastic tablecloth by the edges. The teacher puts a little water on it and a piece of crepe paper. We can rock the cloth gently to the music and the crepe paper will colour the water.

• Ask the children to cut coloured paper circles (buy stickers or make them yourself) in halves. They should stick them side by side; the rounded side up and the hollow side down, and then use a writing implement to draw the wavy movements along them. 'Humpety dumpety bumpety bump' is sung or recited in a variety of sounds and then played with the music. Alternatively, all kinds of pictures of cuddly toys can be cut out of magazines and stuck on paper with krongelidong and train loops or wavy humpety dumpety movements drawn around them. Don't forget the sounds or switch on the music.

Yoyo and Meema are playing in the garden; they are playing cat and mouse. Yoyo is the cat and Meema is the mouse. Meema can run very fast and keeps hiding behind the bushes. Yoyo doesn't like it! He can't find her anywhere.

'I won't play anymore,' he shouts at the top of his voice until Meema finally reappears.

'Okay, shall we play another game?' asks Meema. Yoyo wants to be the lion and creeps through the bushes. Pippa, the cat, thinks it is fun and keeps up with him.

'You must roar, don't forget,' says Meema, 'because I am a little lion cub and otherwise I will lose you.'

Yoyo is very good at roaring and the lady next door peeps over the hedge to see what is going on. She has two ice creams in paper cups with umbrellas on top. What a nice surprise!

'Here you are, little roaring lions,' she says, 'here are two ice creams for you, they were left over.'

'Thank you very much,' they both say and sit down in the grass with their ice creams.

'Look this is an umbrella,' says Meema. In hot countries they use umbrellas because the sun burns. This is what she has learnt at school. She points her umbrella upwards.

'No, you're wrong, it's raining Meema, the grass is getting wet,' says Yoyo. How is that possible? Where has the rain suddenly come from?

'Look up quickly,' says the neighbour, 'there's a rainbow.' What beautiful bright colours!

But it is beginning to pour and Yoyo and Meema run inside. They look for scarves in the dressing-up box, because now they want to play rainbows. Can you imagine how they will play rainbows?

Song

Red and blue
And green and violet,
Now look here, my jacket is wet
Many colours, long and wide,
I am swaying left and right.
Look at the rainbow up in the sky, so high, let's fly,
Away up in the sky. (4x)

Words	Movements	
Red and yell- ow blue and in- di- go	*Forming arched movements with arms up in the air*	
Here comes the rain and there goes the sun	*Expressing raindrops with hands and wrists*	
Ma- ny col- ours, long and wide I am sway- ing left and right	*Arched movements with arms and entire body*	
Look at the rainbow up in the sky so high, let's fly	*Tiptoeing and stretching up your arms as far as you can*	
A- way up in the sky (4x)	*Looking up and jumping up and down on the spot* *Sitting: stamp your feet to the rhythm*	
Red and blue and green and violet	*Form arches with scarves in the air*	
Now look here my jacket is wet	*Form arches with scarves in the air*	
Many colours long and wide I am swaying left and right	*Form arches with scarves and your whole body*	
Look at the rainbow up in the sky So high, let's fly	*Stand on tiptoes and wave the scarves*	
A- way up in the sky	*Look up and jump in your space.* *Sitting: stamp your feet to the rhythm of the music*	

Scrimbling	Illustrations
Form arches with both hands *The arches (pieces of chalk) can 'kiss' each other in opposite directions*	
Draw rain-dots everywhere	
Form arches with both hands	
Tiptoe while holding the pieces of chalk and stretch up your arms, or draw lines upward	
Draw dots or dashes upward	
Without music: form coloured arches *With music: consolidate the arches*	
Continue forming arches	
Continue forming arches	
Stand on tiptoes with the pieces of chalk still in your hands	
Stipple	

Expressions on the scrimbling surface

Foundation movement: arches from side to side

We will divide one or two fair sized circles in two by drawing a flat line across them and we will then pass to and fro over the top half/halves with our fingers or with pieces of chalk in a semi-circular manner.
We could accompany this by singing this line from the song: 'many colours long and wide ...'

Then we make the arches run from right to left so that the arches cross each other back and forth. This swaying movement will let the arches 'walk'.

Then we place a couple of arches in a line and bounce over them like rabbits while saying out loud: hop, hop, hop!

We may apply the same three steps to the lower half of the circle or circles:
* running your fingers or pieces of chalk along the boat or the two boats
* rocking the boats to the left or to the right
* making a line of several boats, until it looks like a garland

Then we sing a lullaby, for example: 'Row, row, row the boat ...'
The upper half of the body sways along.
The swaying movement recurs in the fun fair theme of the Watermill.
The foundation movements of arches and boats will help make it easier to write the letters m, n, h, and u, v, w and y later on with less effort, a lighter pressure and less loss of energy.

Theme Play

• We walk up and down the hall or stamp our feet while sitting down; when the teacher rings a bell, the children wave their arms high up in the air. We could also first rock our heads from side to side, followed by our hands and next with our entire body. We can do this either standing, sitting or lying down.

• Two children form an arch holding their hands against each other. We play games by walking or crawling under the arches.

• One child represents the rainbow by making an arch with her body down to the ground. The other children place the scarves on top of her one by one.

• The teacher draws a big arch on the self-made boards and the children wipe out their arches with movements from side to side, wet or dry.

• Draw little umbrellas, cut them out and stick them onto a stick.

• You might be able to buy some mesh 'food umbrellas', which protect food from flies. Cover them with a scarf and hide objects under them (arch = closed, hidden). Turn over the umbrella and put light objects in it, and if you like allow it to float in an inflatable swimming pool (boat = openness, free to pick up again). We can also hang an umbrella from a pulley from the ceiling to lay objects in it and thus hide them. We will take them out when we lower the umbrella. You could also invent guessing games.

• Play outside with a garden hose and umbrella.

Story

Matching Theme Funfair: Dear Sun, Dear Moon

It has stopped raining and Yoyo and Meema want to go out into the garden to play.

'Just look at that enormous puddle,' says Yoyo and he begins to stamp in it with his bare feet.

'Splash, splash!' says Yoyo and at first Meema jumps away, but then she joins in. What a lot of fun they are having and it makes them feel quite hot. The sun is coming out again and the sunrays tickle their faces. Now they are splashing about with their hands in the water and the water feels nice and warm too.

'Thank you dear sun,' says Meema, 'for warming up the water. Keep on shining because maybe we will be able to go to the beach tomorrow.' It has rained heavily.

They take a stick and stir the puddle and make all kinds of wriggly tracks in the wet soil. Yoyo also draws some straight lines and turns the puddle into a little sun. Meema is feeling too hot and finds a new puddle in the shade of the trees.

'Look Yoyo, a little worm,' she calls out. A tiny worm is wriggling in the water and it climbs up Meema's stick. Pippa, the cat, has also seen it. She is playing in the water with her paw but she can't get hold of the worm.

'Come here, put on these hats,' says Mum, and she brings out a red and a blue hat. The sun feels quite hot.

'I am going to fold a hat out of paper,' says Yoyo. Yesterday he learnt how to make one at school. Meema puts a plastic bowl on her head because she likes it more than her hat.

Song

Words	Movements
Li- ttle sun, li- ttle sun, shine in and out Li- ttle sun, li- ttle sun, shine out and in	*We will move the arms away from the body and back again and turn around*
Li- ttle sun, li- ttle sun, shine in and out Li- ttle sun, li- ttle sun, shine out and in	*Repeat*
Shine ev- e- ry day and on my way And shine while I am out at play	*Stretch your arms and turn around*
Shi- ne and sh- ine and sh- ine every day	*Repeat*
I'm run- ning out to go and play (4x)	*Run without moving or run away* *Sitting: stamp your feet on the spot*

Scrimbling	Illustrations
Drawing circles and drawing lines inward and outward	
Repeat	
Draw dots or dashes close to the circle	
Scrimbling around	
Draw dots and dashes everywhere	

Expressions on the scrimbling surface

Foundation movement: radiate in and out from a dot or circle

We could also call this theme a 'circle of light'. In preparation we create round movements in the air with our whole body or only with our arms (upright circles or flat circles, both are possible). On the surface we form one circle with both hands close together, or two at the same time, one with our left and one with our right hand. Now we can turn on the music and sing the beginning of the song together and repeat it several times:
'Little sun, little sun, shine in and out,
Little sun, little sun, shine in and out.'
Of course we will draw long lines out, or in.
In circle games, we focus on the child in the centre. In addition we could also put a dot in the centre and thus symbolise the sense of self. We will experience the interaction between ourselves and others or our surroundings by this inward and outward radiation. Without music we could also do this by blowing and sucking to pay attention to our breathing.
Instead of long lines inward and outward we could also create smoke garlands, such as the Toy Train or Air Train, or waves such as in the Little Water Shute or the Big Water Shute. Of course we will do this on a big sheet of paper by reinforcing different colours over each other.
We can continually add another colour of paint from a bottle or a pipette on a wet surface.

Theme Play

• Represent sunrays beaming out and in while standing, lying down or sitting. We can also try to breathe in and out as long as possible.

• Draw a circle on the floor and when the music is set to 'pause', we walk into the circle.

• Try and invent all kinds of games with a child standing in the centre. If you have a Write Dance table with a hole cut in the centre (see Introduction) then this should be an appropriate theme for using it.

• Make sunrays inward and outward with paint, shaving foam, bath foam and so on.

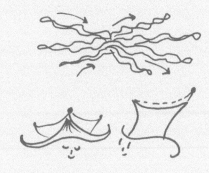

• Make a variety of headgear out of newspapers, plastic, cardboard or material and try and express it in the song.

Story

Yoyo and Meema are playing on their grandma's and grandpa's big terrace. Yoyo has found a branch of willow. He is the leader of the brass band. His strides are stiff and he waves his branch from side to side.

'Tootah toot toot,' shouts Meema with her hands to her mouth. The branch becomes weak and breaks with all the waving about.

'I don't like this game anymore,' says Yoyo.

'Yes Yoyo, look, you can turn it into a complete circle; now it is a hoop.' Meema holds both ends close together and shows him.

'Shall we play circus? You are a puppy, just jump through.' Yoyo jumps and falls flat on his face. He cries and is very cross with Meema.

'Now my branch has snapped completely,' he says angrily and he runs away quickly and stamps his feet.

But a minute later he is back again and says, 'I want to be a brass band leader.' He puts on Grandpa's cap which is lying on a chair. Meema gathers small branches with leaves and quickly picks some daisies on the lawn.

'And look! I am one of those girls with a short skirt, waving lots of feathers around.'

She cheerfully hops and skips around the garden, but Yoyo continues to step slowly, keeping his back and arms very stiff and meanwhile looking for a new branch.

Song

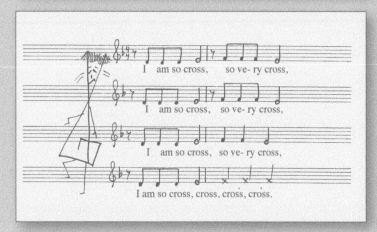

Words	Movements
My back is very straight My back is very straight My back is very straight My back is straight, straight, straight	*We are walking with a straight back, hands tight against the body or straight up in the air*
I'm like a krong- e- li- dong I slith- er like a worm I'm like a kring- e- li- dong I slith- er like a worm	*The teacher first shows a 'krongelidong': which is anything that can bend, bending your body, arms, wrists, ankles, knees, neck, back, if possible all together! Then the children copy*
I am so cross, so ve- ry cross I am so cross, so ve- ry cross I am so cross, so very cross I am so cross, cross, cross, cross!	*We make angry faces, angry fists and stamp our way down the hall, or stamp while we are sitting in our places, to the rhythm of the music*
I am so ve- ry ha- ppy, as ha- ppy as can be Catch me, catch me, if you can, dance a dance, a dance with me I am so ve- ry ha- ppy, as ha- ppy as can be Catch me, catch me, if you can, dance along with me	*We hop, dance, roll, tumble or jump on our own or together down the hall.* *Sitting: dance on a chair*

Scrimbling	Illustrations
Draw upright lines, up and down	
Draw krongelidongs everywhere, with loops in a variety of directions	
Draw strong lines and right angles	
Scrimbling, drawing lines and dots without constraint	
Draw upright lines, up and down	

Expressions on the scrimbling surface

Foundation movement: straight lines and loops, strong and playful movements

Four verses, each with a title that speaks for itself.

Straight: as we experienced in The Staircase and The Procession, marching time gives control and physical coordination, but it also gives a sense of discipline, reinforcement and assertiveness. We could first accompany this verse with the drum and thus set different rhythms.

Bent: the krongelidong-movements of Kringeli-krangeli and My Dinky Car. Round lines give a sense of fluidity, fullness and softness.

Angry: who can make the angriest face? Tense all your facial muscles! We now use extra pressure with the pieces of chalk and draw the ragged teeth of a shark, lion or giant.

Happy: dashes, dots, squiggles, loops or circles: everything is good, nothing is wrong!

Theme Play

• While following each other in a line we repeat the actions that accompany the song. When sitting or lying down we stretch and bend our arms and legs and think of suitable sounds.

• Coloured pipe-cleaners can be left straight or bent to make figures. Use dough or clay to make straight rolls, count them and then join them together to make some meandering figures or suns.

• Contrasts: we play with hard and soft materials, thick and thin, big and small; we make something turn quickly or slowly.

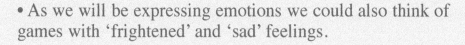

• As we will be expressing emotions we could also think of games with 'frightened' and 'sad' feelings.

Funfair

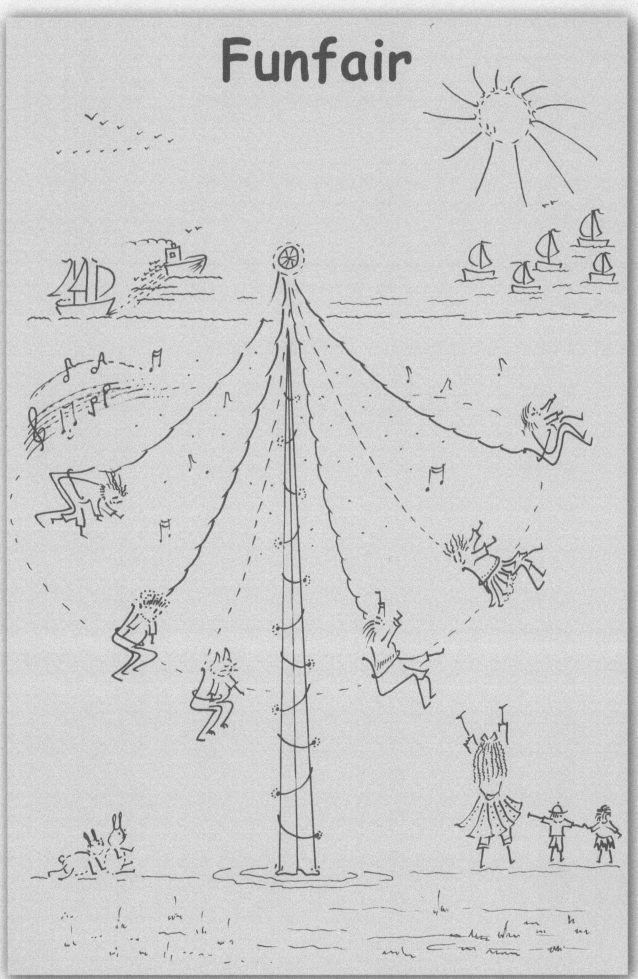

Story and Song

Matching Theme Home: Sandyhill

Yoyo and Meema are going to the funfair with their Dad. They enter through a big gateway with lights. There is a lot of music and lots of noise and Meema skips with excitement while Yoyo strides ahead holding his Dad's hand.

'Look, that's the shooting gallery,' says Dad, 'it might be too difficult for you, but we could go to the marquee where they throw balls.' They pass under the enormous roller-coaster. The roller-coaster cars make a screeching noise and Meema ducks down.

'Look, that's new,' says Yoyo and he points up at a very high post which shoots people up in a cabin, after which they drop down very, very, very quickly. The girls' long hair flies up in the air. They walk on a little and arrive at the tent with little watermills. It is more suitable for little children.

'Shall we stop here?' asks Meema and Yoyo and Daddy like it, too. There are five watermills in a row and there are three other children also choosing a watermill. The man gives them a big bucket of water and a small bucket or a watering can.

'You should take as much water as you can out of the big bucket with your little bucket and pour it into the trays, otherwise it will not turn,' says the man. Yoyo's mill is beginning to slow down and he adds more water. Meema has dropped her watering can, but it doesn't matter. The man has filled it up with water. The mill belonging to a girl called Emma is now turning very fast because she is pouring a lot of water into it. It is fun seeing all those turning mills. The children find all their water has gone and Yoyo and Meema return to their Dad.

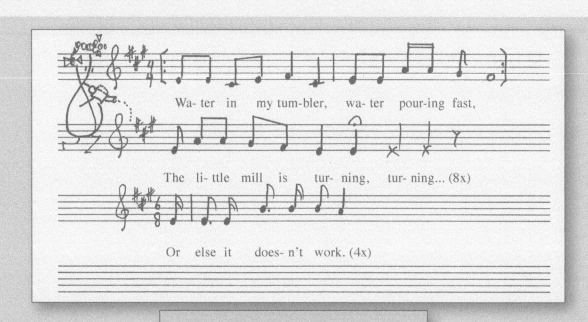

Water from my bucket,
Water pouring fast,
Water from my bucket,
Water pouring fast,
The little mill is turning,
Turning… (8x)
And else it doesn't work. (4x)

Words	Movements
Wa- ter in my tum-bler wa-ter pour-ing fast Wa- ter in my tum-bler wa-ter pour-ing fast	*Make pouring movements*
The li- ttle mill is tur- ning tur- ning... (8x)	*Turn your wrists round each other and/or turn round in your place*
And else it does- n't work (4x)	*Jump and shake your head*
Water from my bucket Water pouring fast Water from my bucket Water pouring fast	*Pretend you are pouring water from a bucket*
The li- ttle mill is tur- ning Tur- ning... (8x)	*Turn your wrists round each other and/or turn round in your place*
And else it does- n't work (4x)	*Jump and shake your head*

Scrimbling	Illustrations
Quarter circles, or simply make arches from side to side	
Circling around	
Jumping, stippling, shaking your head and drawing lines from side to side	
Quarter circles or arches from side to side	
Circling around	
Jumping, stippling, shaking your head and drawing lines from side to side	

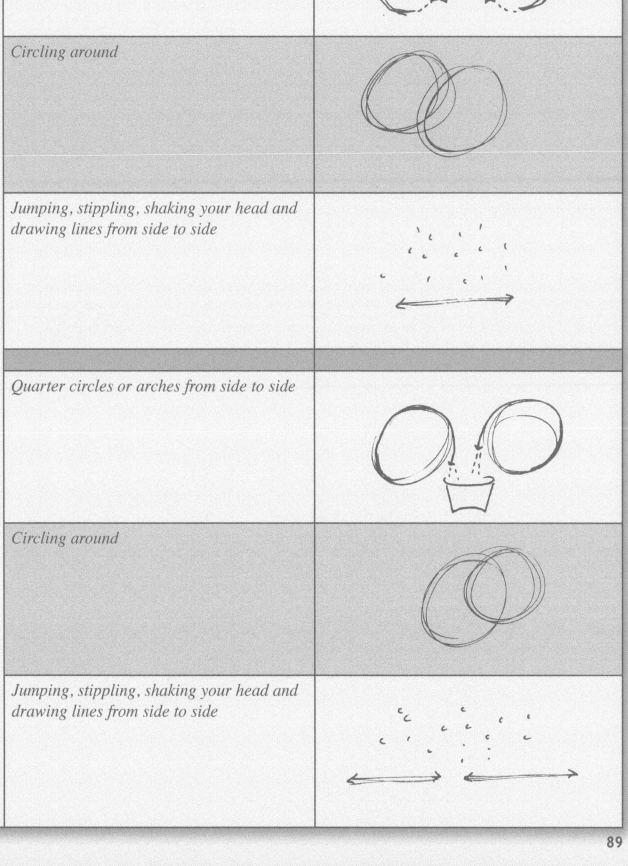

Theme Play

• Play with buckets, trays, beakers and coloured water thickened with glue. Make a mark on a piece of plastic and arrange for the 'mark train' to come along (see The Toy Train). It is possible to replace thickened water with sand, beads, marbles and so on.

• Cover bowls with paper-mache and paint them when they're dry. These bowls are hollow. Bigger plastic bowls can be used for hats; they are round.

• Fill a strong freezer bag with water and tie it. Cut a tiny point off and put it in a bucket after use. We scrimble on a big plastic sheet and with the small jet of water we try to make more lines. Next dry everything with your hands or cloths. You could replace water with fine play sand.

• Invent games that combine hiding and water. Place a little object in a big bucket and pour a little black coloured water over it. The object has disappeared. If we continue to pour clear water over it the object will reappear!

Story and Song

Matching Theme Home: Kringeli-krangeli

Yoyo has thrown many balls in the marquee. He found it very difficult. Two out of ten balls passed through the hole, which was very good. Meema threw some balls at the tins, but she didn't hit any and started to cry. Nevertheless both of them were allowed to choose a small prize. Yoyo chose a green lollypop and Meema a red one. They walk on very slowly and stop to look around.

'Look those are dinky dodgem cars,' says Dad. There are six of them and Yoyo gets in a blue one and Meema in a green one. They look like shoes and have cute faces. They both pop a coin in the slot and the cars start off. All you have to do is steer – how exciting.

'Mind your steering Meema,' says Dad, because Meema looks in all directions except straight ahead. Yoyo is quite good at it and has passed his Dad three times. He is really proud and imagines he is a lorry driver. Suddenly all the cars stop.

'Can we have another go?' asks Yoyo and they are given another coin to put in the slot.

'I am going to overtake you,' shouts Yoyo, but Meema doesn't mind, she is pretending her white car is a brand new trainer.

My dinky car, my dinky car,
I'm twisting around on the ground.
This nice little car is very black…
It's racing down the track. (2x)

My dinky car, my dinky car,
I'm twisting around on the ground.
This nice little car is very white…
And look I'm sitting tight. (4x)

91

Words	Movement
My din- ky car, my din- ky car I'm twist-ing a-round on the ground	*Pretend you are driving your car*
This nice li- ttle car is ve- ry blue…	*Pause the music: we look for a blue colour anywhere* *(The music continues)*
And just looks like a shoe (2x)	*Jumping and pointing at your shoes*
My din- ky car, my din- ky car I'm twist-ing a-round on the ground	*Steering motions*
This nice little car is very black…	*Pause the music: we look for a black colour anywhere* *(The music continues)*
It's racing down the track (2x)	*Wave your arm in any direction and run around*
My din- ky car, my din- ky car I'm twist-ing a-round on the ground	*Steering motions*
This nice little car is very white…	*Pause the music: we look for white anywhere or point at teeth* *(The music continues)*
And look I'm sitting tight (4x)	*Sit 'proudly' at your wheel and firmly move your head from side to side*

Scrimbling	Illustrations
'Ride' across the writing surface with blue fingers or pieces of chalk	
Make a blue 'scrimble track' with matching sounds Or: scrimble a shoe	
Scrimble across the 'scrimble track' or the shoe	
'Ride' across the surface with black fingers or pieces of chalk	
Make a black 'scrimble track' with matching sounds	
'Ride' fast across the surface	
'Ride' across the surface with both hands	
Finger dance across the 'scrimble tracks'	
Circle around with a smile on your face	

Theme Play

• 'Drive' a little car along a wriggly road drawn in chalk. Change direction, alone or together, we meet each other, avoid each other, follow each other, bump into each other, speed up, slow down and so on.

• In the sand you can make imprints of toy cars or other vehicles.

• We can also sing other transport songs, such as 'The Wheels on the Bus'.

• Run a car along your own body or somebody else's: fast, slow, with more or less pressure. One child is lying on his tummy on the floor. Another child or teacher makes the vehicle jump like a flea or fly through the air like a fly and then it makes a surprise landing on a leg or on an upper arm… Sounds and sudden surprises make it more exciting!

Story and Song

Matching Theme Home: Pat-a-cake

Isn't it a beautiful old-fashioned merry-go-round at the funfair? The man looking after the merry-go-round proudly tells them that his grandpa bought it and that it is one hundred years old today. That is why everybody is presented with a small ice cream before getting on. There is a long staircase to the merry-go-round and you have to go up at least six steps. Yoyo chooses to sit on the elephant. Meema is sitting on a horse and the girl called Emma is back again. She is sitting on a giraffe that can bend its knees when the merry-go-round begins to turn. Next it goes up and down. Yoyo and Meema are sitting so high up that they can see the beach and the sea in the distance.

    'Dad, our sand hill is still there,' shouts Yoyo.

    'Hurray, the sea hasn't washed it away yet,' exclaims Meema.

The merry-go-round has begun to turn. Meema sings the song her teacher has taught her: 'Hold horsy tight, my horse has had a fright…'

    'Tootah toot toot,' says Yoyo's elephant when he pushes a button behind the elephant's ear. But the giraffe doesn't say anything, it only bends its knees and leaves Emma's long hair waving in the wind. It is beginning to go dark, but they don't have to go home yet.

Hold horsy tight, my horse has had a fright. (2x)

Turn me round and round once more

And put me on the floor.

Tootah toot toot,
This really is a hoot.
Tootah toot toot,
This really is a hoot.
My arm is straight, my arm is bent
And round the bend we went.

Hip, hip, hooray,
I see my hill of sand
Hip, hip, hooray,
I see my hill of sand.
Wash it up ashore big sea,
But leave my hill to me.

Words	Movements
Hold horsy tight My horse has had a fright Hold horsy tight My horse has had a fright	*All of you gallop in a big circle*
Turn me round and round once more	*Turn round in your place*
And put me on the floor	*Sit down*
Tootah toot toot This really is a hoot Tootah toot toot This really is a hoot	*Make hooting movements with one hand in front of your mouth*
My arm is straight, my arm is bent	*Stretch out an arm and bend it back again*
And round the bend we went	*Turn round in your place*
Hip, hip, hooray	*Stretch out both arms in the air*
I see my hill of sand	*Keep one hand over your eyes and look out*
Hip, hip, hooray	*Stretch out both arms in the air*
I see my hill of sand	*Keep one hand over your eyes and look out*
Wash it up ashore big sea	*Make wavy movements with your arms*
But leave my hill to me	*Continue making wavy movements*

Scrimbling	Illustrations
Jump while stippling	
Circle around	
Keep hold of the pieces of chalk and sit down quickly on the chair or on the floor	
Draw long lines	
Draw slanting or semi-circular lines	
Circling around	
Jump and stipple	
Jump and stipple	
Jump and stipple	
Jump and stipple	
Scrimble waves	
Scrimble waves	

Theme Play

• We walk round a hoop on the floor to the rhythm of the music and when the music is set to pause, we stop a moment. Alternatively, scatter some sponges round the hall and when the music stops all the children try and find a sponge.

• We put five or six hoops in the classroom and in the middle we see the merry-go-round man. He takes tickets or hands out ice creams.

• The teacher takes some chalk and draws an enormous circle on the floor helped by the children. Tie a piece of chalk to a piece of string about a metre long and tie a loop at the other end. One child holds the end with the loop and the teacher turns round with the chalk like a compass. The child has been closed in and has now become a merry-go-round herself.

• The older children can use the string to play 'Hold Horsy Tight'.

Story and Song

Matching Theme Home: The Staircase

They can hear music in the distance.

'It's the brass band,' says Dad. 'Let's stand next to the cake stall and we will see them pass by.'

'Isn't it exciting, what will the musicians' costumes be like?', thinks Meema. More people join her and they all wait for the band to pass by.

Beat the drum! Beat the drum. Beat the big big drum. Everybody can hear it clearly. Tootatoot-toot, hear the trumpet hoot.

Meema is clinging onto her Dad because she is a little afraid. The music is getting louder. They are coming round the corner. Meema can see the girls wearing short green skirts. Holding her father's hand tightly she hops and skips to the music in her place. She is no longer tired, in fact she is feeling quite excited. The boys are wearing long trousers with yellow stripes down the sides.

'Can we walk along?' Yoyo asks, and he, too, is holding Dad's hand tightly.

The three of them are marching to the rhythm. The big drum is still beating loudly. And the trumpet is still hooting… tootatoot-toot. The procession proceeds under the big gateway of the funfair and Yoyo and Meema wave to the people in the procession.

'Bye, very big drum,' says Yoyo.

'Bye, tootatoot-toot,' shouts Meema.

Tootatoot-toot	The sound of the very big drum.	Beat the drum
Tootatoot-toot	Meema hops hippety hop	Beat the drum
Hear my trumpet hoot.	Yoyo slides steppety step	Come and follow the drum.
Beat the drum	Meema hops hippety hop	
Beat the drum	Yoyo slides steppety step.	Beat the drum
		Beat the drum
		Come and follow the drum.

Words	Movements
Beat the drum, beat the drum Beat the big big drum Beat the drum, beat the drum Beat the big big drum	*We pretend we are beating a big drum and say out loud 'Beat the drum'*
Boys and girls come out to play	*Arms welcome boys and girls*
Girls and lads play on the way	*Slide your hands slowly along you legs from your hips downward past your knees*
Boys and girls come out to play Girls and lads play on the way	*Jump and hop in your place*
Beat the drum, beat the drum Come and follow the drum	*Drum, step and speak: 'Beat the drum'*
Beat the drum, beat the drum Come and follow the drum	*Repeat*
Tootatoot-toot tootatoot-toot Hear my trumpet hoot	*One hand at your mouth, bend the other arm and stretch*
Beat the drum, beat the drum The sound of the very big drum	*Drum, step and speak: 'Beat the drum'*
Meema hops hippety hop	*Jump and skip*
Yoyo slides steppety step	*Make big, long strides Sitting: Raise your knees up high*
Meema hops hippety hop Yoyo slides steppety step	*Repeat*
Beat the drum, beat the drum	*Drum*
Come and follow the drum	*Drum*
Beat the drum, beat the drum Come and follow the drum	*Repeat*

Scrimbling	Illustrations
Stipple and draw dashes with two hands to the rhythm of the music or draw squares	
Draw lines towards you	
Stipple	
Repeat	
Draw dots and dashes to the rhythm of the music	
Repeat	
Draw slanting lines with two hands, up and down	
Draw dots and dashes to the rhythm of the music or draw squares	
Draw small, quick 'skipping' dashes	
Draw long lines	
Repeat	
Draw dots and lines or squares	
Long lines downward	
Repeat	

Theme Play

• The teacher beats the drum in a marching rhythm and the children walk in time with the beat. Alternate slow and quick drum beats. We take big steps on the slow beats and can pretend we are going upstairs.

• Let the children improvise and beat all kinds of things. The teacher has a little bell, a horn or some other kind of instrument. All the children are drumming and when the teacher gives them a sign they stop, or continue.

• Let the boys and girls dance round the room and play the song, 'I am so very happy'. Next ask them to walk around pretending to be cross. Boys and girls change expressions in turn.

• We can experiment with line formations: follow each other in a line, and when the teacher gives a sign the one at the front walks to the back or we walk in pairs, make a wriggly track, walk in a circle and so on.

• Repeat games with round and straight movements.

Story and Song

Matching Theme Home: The Toy Train

'Toot toot!' says the funfair train. It is travelling along very high tracks in the air and has a cute face. When it travels its eyes open and shut. They are its lights. Yoyo tries to copy the movement with his eyes, but it isn't easy at all. There are so many wheels that it looks like a thousand.

'Just get in and then we will travel high up through the air and it doesn't cost anything at all,' says the air train conductor.
The three of them climb up another very long staircase with as many as ten steps. Meema's legs feel a little tired, but fortunately they are almost there. They get in and the guard closes all the doors firmly with a key.

'Right, now nobody can fall out,' says Dad. They can clearly see the sea and the beach.
Yoyo and Meema's sand hill is far too far away, but they can see lots of windsurfers and kite surfers. One of the surfers takes an enormous leap up in the air.

'Did you see that Meema?' Yoyo gives her a nudge, but Meema was looking in the opposite direction. She saw a… Yes, what did she see? The air train is slowing down now.

'Toooot, toooot!' says the whistle and the train switches its headlight-eyes on and off.

Puffa, puffa, puffa, puffa, fun
ahead,
No, we don't want to go to bed.
Puffa, puffa, puffa, puffa, fun
ahead,
No, we don't want to go to bed.
Open the door, shut the door,
My train rolls along the floor.

Words	Movements
Puff- a, puff- a, puff- a, puff- a, fun a- head	*Make loops of smoke in the air with both hands*
No, we don't want to go to bed	*Shake your head slowly*
The light goes on	*Open your eyes and/or spread your fingers wide*
Off it goes	*Close your eyes and/or clench fingers into fists*
The light goes on, off it goes	*Repeat*
Toot toot, the whistle blows	*Pretend you are pulling the whistle*
Puff- a, puff- a, puff- a, puff- a, fun a- head	*Make loops of smoke*
No, we don't want to go to bed	*Shake your head slowly*
Open the door	*We pretend to open a door*
Shut the door	*Close the door*
Open the door, shut the door	*Repeat*
My train rolls along the floor	*Walk through the classroom*

Scrimbling	Illustrations
Draw loops across the entire writing surface or along the edges	
Draw flat lines and meanwhile shake your head	
Draw two circles, one with your left hand and one with your right. Pause the music, now make these circles into eyes.	
Draw flat lines or 'little boats' across the eyes with two hands	
Repeat	
Draw long lines downward	
Draw loops along the edges	
Draw flat lines and meanwhile shake your head	
Form quarter circles outward with both hands, to and fro	
Form quarter circles outward with both hands, to and fro	
Repeat	
Draw loops along the edges	

Theme Play

• We will do the same movements and express ourselves in the same way as we did with The Toy Train. What kind of sound does an air train make?

• The marks we made in the field of marks in The Toy Train theme, using confetti and snippets of paper or sand (outside), could represent clouds.

• Maybe the teacher knows some books about other vehicles that travel through the air which he/she can read aloud. Otherwise we will imagine some ourselves. What else can travel through the air? We continually allow our arms and wrists to move in circles.

• If there is a long PE bench available, the children could alternate riding on it on the floor and 'in the air', once again forwards and backwards.

• We place objects on the floor in a line and walk in and out of them in loops.

Story and Song

Matching Theme Home: Tickle Tree

It is growing dark and many of the lights at the funfair are lit. The trees are also lit. One tree has very many little lights: red, blue, green and white. They are flashing on and off. Meema would like to touch all those lights but they are too high up.

The lights are flashing on and off, clip, clop. Yoyo closes one of his eyes so that he can have a better view of that one little red light and he pretends he can reach it. Snatch, snatch, snatch is the movement he makes with his hands.

'Tomorrow I am going to draw a tree with lots of coloured specks in it,' he tells his Dad.

'Are you also planning to draw the big drum in the procession?' asks Dad, but Yoyo doesn't know yet. Those dotted lights are much easier. Now he can see a nice lady next to the tree who is also inspecting the lights.

'If you come and stand here, a bit further away from the noise, you can hear the song coming from the tree,' says the lady. The three of them follow the dear old lady. Now they can hear the tree sing: 'All the little lights in the tree, I see you and you see me.' It makes Yoyo and Meema laugh and Dad lifts them up high in turn, but the lights are still too far away.

'Thank you,' says Dad to the lady. Yoyo will now be able to sing this song tomorrow when he draws the dotted lights in his tree.

'I can also draw a big forest,' says Yoyo to the old lady and she gives him a kind smile and walks on.

All the little lights in the tree-ee,

I see you and you see me-e.

Cli- pper, cli- pper, cli- pper, clip, clop clop.

Red and blue and green and whi-ite,
All the little lights are so bri-ight.
Clipper, clipper, clipper, clip,
Clop clop.

Words	Movements
All the little lights in the tree-ee I see you and you see me-e	*Using two index fingers first point to another child, then to yourself*
Cli- pper, cli- pper, cli- pper, clip	*Shake your entire body*
Clop clop!	*Make fists*
Red and blue and green and whi-ite	*Pinch the air with your thumb and fingers and hop up and down a little*
All the little lights are so bri-ight	*Open your eyes wide*
Clipper, clipper, clipper, clip	*Quick grabbing movements*
Clop clop!	*Make fists*
All the little lights in the tree-ee	*Using two index fingers first point to*

Scrimbling	Illustrations
In advance we drew a simple tree. Now we draw dots in the tree to the rhythm of the music	
Stipple	
Draw a line with your left hand and a line with your right hand to the rhythm	
Pause the music: in the tree we first draw blue and yellow, followed by green dots (The music continues)	
Pause the music: hands down on the surface and stand up and sit down (or stand) several times and stand again (or sit down) (The music plays on)	
Fast stippling*	
Draw two firm lines, one with your left hand and one with your right hand	

*variation to 'clipper clipper clipper clip': pause the music: we use a bell; each time the bell sounds, we change from stippling in the air to stippling on the surface and in reverse.

Theme Play

• Tap your own body or somebody else's gently with your fingertips. That is the way to express the flashing lights.

• Move hands and fingers around in shaving foam and scrimble. Use a pipette to add coloured drops. They can represent lights that slowly switch on and off.

• We can make a festive tree by sticking confetti, snippets of paper or cloth, rice or cotton wool balls to your 'scrimble tree'.

Story and Song

Matching Theme Home: Little Water Shute

It is almost completely dark at the funfair and it still feels quite warm. Yoyo and Meema have had two ice creams and they are still feeling hot. They are wandering round and think they have seen everything at the funfair. But then…

'Look, there's a water shute,' shouts Yoyo and runs on ahead. There are little boats which can take three people. Each boat looks like a fish. Yoyo, Meema and Dad get into the blue dolphin. Right in front of them there is a little yellow boat with the face of a shark. It looks very angry and has a lot of big white teeth. A mother with two heavy boys gets into the shark boat. Oh, how it wobbles. The mother gets a shock, but laughs nevertheless.

The boats are pulled up by a chain, which is very exciting. Yoyo and Meema look in all directions and can see all kinds of things, the cake stall, the merry-go-round, the dinky cars and the sea and the beach.

'Hold on tight, we have almost reached the top,' says Dad. The boat stops. The shark boat with the mother and two little boys has also stopped.

'I find this very scary,' they hear the mother call out.

'I will hold on to you, Mum,' says the biggest boy. He might be nine years old and he looks very strong. And then the shark boat swoops down at high speed with the mother and two boys. They hear the mother screaming at the top of her voice and they see that they have reached the bottom.

'Splash, splaaaaash,' says the water. Now it is Yoyo's and Meema's turn.

'Wow,' cries Yoyo, 'it is going terribly fast.' Meema keeps her eyes tightly shut.

'Splash, splosh, woosh,' says the water. They, too, went down very fast and the three of them are soaking wet.

'Great, that is just what we needed,' says Dad. They decide to go down again but this time they have to queue in a long line because many people have joined feeling hot and wanting to cool down in the boats on the water shute.

Rick-e- ty crick-e- ty boat green and blue,

I'd like to go for a row with you.

Spatter and splatter I'm not ready yet,

Look the boat made me terribly wet.

Dippety doppety dippety day,
Oh, there's so much fun today.
Move along and stand in a line,
Hurray it's now my second time.

Words	Movements
Rick- e- ty crick- e- ty boat green and blue	*Arms and body move to and fro in wavy movements*
I'd like to go for a row with you	*Point to each other or continue to 'make waves'*
Spatter and splatter I'm not ready yet	*We pretend we are shaking water off our hands*
Look, the boat made me terribly wet	*Turn wrists and palms upward or stroke your whole body with your hands*
Dippety doppety dippety day	*Arms and body move like waves*
Oh, there's so much fun today	*Hold your hands against your cheeks and move your head to and fro with a smiling face*
Move along and stand in a line	*Make pushing movements around you with two hands and give yourself plenty of space. Pause the music: the children quickly move into a line behind each other. (The music continues)*
Hurray it's now my second time!	*Keep arms wide in the air and walk around*

Scrimbling	Illustrations
Scrimble waves to and fro *Pause the music: we will draw small circles on the surface so that we can create waves around them. We say out loud: 'And over and under' or Rickety Crickety'* *(The music continues)*	
Keep creating 'waves'	
Pause the music: Splash the surface with toothbrushes and water. *Then continue creating 'waves' with your fingers*	
Wrists and palms turn upward, holding pieces of chalk in your hands	
Scrimble waves	
Draw flat lines and move your head with a smiling face to and fro	
Draw long lines away from you and turn your wrists upward when 'waiting' and 'standing'	
Draw long lines upwards and continue the movements up in the air	

Theme Play

• Think of different ways to make a (wavy) water shute. For example, stick empty packets of fruit juice together, fixing them on a raised platform so the water can run down into a tub. Make a thin wallpaper paste, put it in a beaker with acorns, chestnuts or other items and let it slide down.

• Have any of the children been down the big slide with their father, mother, brother or sister, and what did it feel like? What happens to the water when you crash down the slide with a big splash?

• We will fold boats out of paper and let them sail.

• A big sheet in the centre. Each child walks round the room to the music with their cuddlies. The cuddly toys could also make rolling movements to the music. When the music stops everybody places their cuddly toys on the sheet. They are a little tired and we tuck them in to go to sleep.

• Put a bit of bath foam (preferably blue) on a big sheet of plastic. We are washing the cuddlies! Next we dry them with cloths and sponges.

Story and Song

Matching Theme Home: The Rainbow

Yoyo begins to yawn with his mouth wide open, it's ten o'clock in the evening. Yoyo and Meema have never before gone to bed at that time, but it is holiday time so they don't have to get up early tomorrow morning to go to school. Meema asks if Dad will carry her, but Dad is tired, too, and so they decide to go home. Mum has already rung Dad's mobile because she was getting rather worried. Yoyo wanted to tell her everything immediately, but Mum replied that she was quite happy to wait until they got home. They wander towards the exit.

'Can we have another bag of crisps?' asks Meema, but Dad says it will only make them thirsty and they might find something nice to eat in the car. The gateway at the exit is very big and lit up in beautiful rainbow colours. It looks like a real rainbow. Meema waves her arms from side to side pretending she is a big rainbow herself. Yoyo and Dad have walked on.

'Come on Meema, we really must go now,' says Dad. Meema remembers that Yoyo will want to draw a tree with lights in it. And I will draw a big rainbow, thinks Meema and she hops and skips to catch up with her Dad and brother.

Words	Movements
There is a rainbow high in the sky Many lights and oh so high Many colours, blue and green	*Create arches with your arms stretched high*
More lights than I've ever seen	*Place hands before your eyes*
I must count them over again	*Pause the music: accompany the words with movements by stretching your fingers one by one and 'counting' (The music continues)*
Look, so many in the sky	*Again stretch your fingers one by one and 'count'*
Try and reach them, oh so high	*Grabbing movements in the air while you are on tiptoes*
Here is the gateway in...	*Each child points to their chest*
There is the gateway out...	*Each child points into the distance*
Here is the rainbow red... Shining over my head...	*Big arching movements*
I'm jumping up and down (4x)	*Jump up and down without moving away*

Scrimbling	Illustrations
Create arches with your arms stretched high	
Stipple and count out loud	
Continue to stipple, close your eyes and shake your head	
Stipple along the gateway and count	
Put dashes across all the dots	
Two hands rest together under one arch	
Two hands rest together under the other arch	
Form rainbows (pause the music)	
Stipple while jumping	

Theme Play

• The teacher will place two objects, for example, two drums, a metre apart. The other children will move from one drum to another in a big sweep.

• We will decorate the classroom door with garlands and stick them together into an arch with pieces of blu-tack.

• As we did with round and straight shapes, we now look for arched shapes around us.

Story and Song

Matching Theme Home: Little Sun

Dad starts the car engine. Vroom, is the sound the car makes with Yoyo and Meema in the back.

'Wasn't it a hot day,' says Dad after a while, 'and wasn't it great that the sun warmed up the funfair all day right into the evening?'

'Yes, because otherwise the water on the big water shute would have been far too cold,' says Yoyo.

'Do you think the sun will shine again tomorrow, Dad?' asks Meema.

'I think so,' says Dad, 'because the sun is always shining, but sometimes it doesn't break through the clouds and it is a grey day.'

'And this was a yellow day, wasn't it Dad,' says Meema and she hears Dad's little laugh.

'I suppose so, and what colour is it now Meema?' asks Dad. Meema looks up at the sky which hasn't yet turned completely dark and suddenly she sees the moon.

'Look at the moon,' she cries excitedly, 'it is completely round tonight. Dad, would you mind stopping the car so that I can have a better view?' she asks.
Dad carefully slows down the car and parks the car at the side of the road. The three of them get out and have a look at the moon. The sky is almost completely dark with a little patch of blue and in the distance they can still see a couple of coloured strips of sun.

'Thank you dear moon,' says Meema, ' for being so round tonight and having such a pretty face.'

'Come on,' says Dad, 'we must go home now otherwise Mum will be worried.' They get back into the car and Dad turns the ignition key.

'Vroom,' says the car and Yoyo and Meema fall asleep on their way home.

My dear sun, my dear moon,
My dear sun, my dear moon,
Going home this afternoon.
Thank you sun, thank you moon,
Thank you sun, thank you moon
I will be back, be back, be back,
Be back, be back very soon.

Words	Movements
My dear sun, my dear moon My dear sun, my dear moon	*Draw circles in the air with both arms or only with your wrists and circle around*
Flying home in a big balloon	*Point in the air with both hands*
Thank you sun, thank you moon Thank you, sun thank you moon	*Blow kisses to the sun and moon*
I will be back, be back, be back Be back, be back very soon	*Run in your place or run around.* *Sitting: stamp your feet on the floor*
My dear sun, my dear moon My dear sun, my dear moon	*Again circle around*
Going home this afternoon	*Turn your wrists upward and look sad*
Thank you sun, thank you moon Thank you sun, thank you moon	*Blow hand kisses*
I will be back, be back, be back Be back, be back very soon	*Run or stamp your feet*

Scrimbling	Illustrations
Scrimble around with both hands together or create two separate circles Pause the music: divide the moon in two and scrimble semi-circles. (The music continues)	
Draw long lines	
Draw little dashes everywhere and away from you	
Stipple around and inside the scrimbled suns and moons	
Scrimble around	
Turn your wrists upwards and look sad	
Draw little dashes everywhere and away from you	
Draw little dashes away from you	

Theme Play

• You can apply the same variations as in the Home theme 'Little Sun' here.

• Make a mobile with suns and moons. Ask the children to scrimble and fill a thick piece of paper or card with paint or wax crayons. Once the shapes have been cut out it is possible to draw faces on them.

• Making and scrimbling stars also belong to this theme. We can finger dance and 'draw' the rays of the sun or a star out from the centre on a wet board.

• Play with shaving foam.

NOTES

NOTES

NOTES